Uplifting Moments

Uplifting Moments

Wallace T. Davis

SONCOAST
PUBLISHING

There are no limits to caring ®

ISBN 978-1-953406-03-3

Cover design by Abigail Jackson
Interior graphic by Freepik

Printed in the United States of America

Published by Soncoast Publishing
P.O. Box 1503
Hartselle, AL 35640
www.soncoastpublishing.com

There are no limits to caring ®

For over 20 years, Wallace T. Davis has inspired and motivated people through his Uplifting Moments, carried on four local radio stations during morning drive time. He is also featured on a local CBS affiliate on Sunday mornings.

Some of the best of these Uplifting Moments are collected in this daily devotional to provide you with encouragement, inspiration, and spiritual insight. This book has been published in hopes that your spirit and faith will grow to new heights as you read, meditate, and share these moments with others

There are no limits to caring ®

6

Preface

Uplifting Moments, created to be uplifting for our communities, have been aired on radio stations throughout the Gulf Coast of Alabama, Florida, and Mississippi for the past twenty-one years during daily 60 seconds "drive time." The past four years, a CBS affiliate television station has broadcast these moments on Sunday mornings as well. When I began this outreach, my purpose was for people in our community to understand the values of Volunteers of America and to learn a little about us and hopefully ignite their curiosity to know more. These moments have been effective in creating a connection with the community and opening up conversations and opportunities. God has blessed us, and we are grateful.

Our intentions are to present *Uplifting Moments* in a setting where readers can use it as a part of their daily devotional time. In each reading, there is an appropriate Bible scripture, an uplifting moment, and an opportunity for you to talk with God and, perhaps, a friend.

I am grateful to those who have come along beside me during this journey. When I began to conceptualize this opportunity, George Myers helped me greatly and assisted in recording these moments. John Bell, the radio production manager for *Clear Channel*, was creative, patient, and supportive; he really made an impact! Ralph Mitchell, the production manager for *IHeart Radio,* took us to new levels and taught us how to develop *Uplifting Moments* in our home office studio. I appreciate our staff who worked closely with me at different times—Amanda Gonzales, Brooke Granade, Emily Pate, Laurie Taylor, and Jolyn Castillo. They were all supportive and helpful along the way.

Rob Jackson assisted in the selection of scriptures from the Bible, as well as the selection of *Uplifting Moments* from the past 21 years. I am thankful for his valuable assistance and insight and help in getting the book published.

There are no limits to caring ®

My wife, Barbara, has been by my side throughout this journey. I am grateful for her love, support, insights, work, and who she is to me. She is also my editor; and she did the audio recording of these moments and made them sound much better than reality!

I am thankful for the many people who have inspired and stimulated me along the way to develop these *Uplifting Moments*. There are those I don't know who have contributed to these moments... for you, a special "thank you." It is impossible to acknowledge all those who gave an illustration. Some stories were on the internet or public domain. Others were stories I have picked up through a lifetime of work. It was not my intention to infringe on anyone's copyright but simply to share an uplifting moment of the best I've seen along my way.

Thank you for your support, and I pray that God will use these meditations. Please, use this book by sharing *Uplifting Moments* where God leads you.

Wallace T. Davis

There are no limits to caring ®

Who is Volunteers of America?

Volunteers of America (VOA) was founded in 1896 by Christian social reformers Maud and Ballington Booth as a ministry of service to support America's most vulnerable population. Serving the entire United States, VOA is committed to helping those in need through our Christian faith-based roots in each community. The Southeast affiliate began in October 1980. Information about Volunteers of America can be found on our national website, www.voa.org, or on our local website, www.voase.org.

Volunteers of America's mission is that of reaching and uplifting all people and bringing them to the knowledge and active service of God. By illustrating the presence of God through all that we do, VOA serves people and communities in need and creates opportunities for people to experience the joy of serving others. Volunteers of America measures its success in the positive changes in the lives of individuals and in the communities we serve.

Uplifting Moments gives us an opportunity to share our values and faith and to offer a positive uplifting message. Proceeds from the sale of the book, *Uplifting Moments*, will benefit VOASE's programs and services. You can purchase the book at www.voase.org, by calling (251) 300-3500, or by visiting our corporate office at 1204 Hillcrest Road, Mobile, Alabama, 36695.

Visit our website, www.voase.org, to learn how you can become a part of the marvelous work of VOASE through your service or your financial investment.

There are no limits to caring®

There are no limits to caring® is a tag line, or registered statement, owned by Volunteers of America, Inc. and licensed for use to the local affiliates. We have used this tag line in many publications and statements.

There are no limits to caring ®

In each radio and television spot we share, that's our message: *There are no limits to caring®.* But how is it lived out in the everyday world? What does this statement mean in the real world?

For the spouse who is abused, it may mean that he/she begins to care for self—and move out of a destructive relationship. That may be the first step to finding no limits to caring for self and others.

For the family of the alcoholic, it may mean to engage a professional interventionist to get the family member in treatment. And that is a tough decision on the family, but it is demonstrating… *There are no limits to caring®.*

For the adult child who won't accept responsibility, it may mean letting that person experience the challenges of life without a rescue attempt. It's called tough love. The only problem with tough love is that it is equally tough on the person who gives it. Tough love may be a part of this concept of no limits to caring.

And in our day-to-day lives, we can always find an opportunity to show to another human being that *There are no limits to caring®.* We use this tag line, not to promote guilt trips, but to encourage us to care for one another in our journey of life.

There are no limits to caring ®

Suggestions on Using this Devotional Book

This devotional book is not written to be an intense Bible study but it is written in hopes that it can contribute to your relationship with God as you daily take time to pull away and listen to what God is saying to you right now. God is at work. (Romans 8:28) And we want to be a part of what He is doing. He will tell us if we but listen! Use your Bible. Search for additional scripture and spend time praying. The purpose of this book is to stimulate you in your relationship with God and one another.

1. Set aside definite time to read, pray, and mediate.
2. Read the scripture that is identified at the beginning of each day.
3. Give God time to speak to you from His Word.
4. Look for other scriptures that speak on this topic.
5. Read the uplifting moment. What is it saying to you, right now?
6. What can you gain to put to work this day? How can you serve others?
7. Prayer time. Talk with God as He is right in the room with you.
8. During the day, let this experience speak to you.
9. Share with someone what God has said to you on this day.

There are no limits to caring ®

January 1

*Brothers and sisters . . . one thing I do: Forgetting what is behind
and straining toward what is ahead* (Philippians 3:13, NIV).

Leaving It Behind

Happy New Year – may you have a wonderful New Year. There
are some things best left behind and some things we need to
transfer to the new year.

- We need to leave behind our hurts and pains. We need to forgive
those who wronged us. Wipe the slate clean for the new year.
- We need to leave behind the mistakes and wrongs we have done.
We need to ask for forgiveness of those we have hurt.

However, also for this new year, we need to take with us the
courage to be all that God has created us to be.

- We need to take into this new year our dreams and hopes. We need
to have a determination to be a brother to those who need a brother
or a sister to those who need a sister.
- We need to take into this new year a caring heart, for there are no
limits to caring.

Happy New Year!

There are no limits to caring ®

January 2

Your beginnings will seem humble, so prosperous will your future be (Job 8:7, NIV).

New Beginning

This week is a time for a new beginning! A new year, a new week, a new start. This year, we can work to achieve what we didn't do last year.

From time to time, everyone wants a new beginning. It may be the person who failed a biology class or the person whose marriage has ended or has faced the death of a loved one. Somehow, we wish that we could make the new better than the past.

We have all made mistakes, experienced pain that we hope will go away. But here we are in a new year. Now is the time for a new beginning.

Three questions for this moment: (1) What do I want to learn from my past? (2) What do I want to leave behind? (3) What do I want to achieve in this New Year?

At VOA, we are all about helping people find a new beginning.

There are no limits to caring ®

January 3

Take delight in the Lord, and He will give you the desires of your heart
(Psalm 37:4, ESV).

Dreams and Reality

Do you have a dream for this New Year? I am one who always encourages you to chase your dream...go with your passion...go where your heart leads!

But while you are chasing your dreams, don't forget the realities that don't go away...you have to pay your bills...if you are a father, you must provide for your family. Just because you have a dream doesn't mean that you cease to be a responsible person. Making your dreams become a reality may mean that you chase your dream on the side while being responsible for yourself, your family, and those who depend on you.

Sometimes our dreams don't add up! No matter what we do, we can't make our dreams become reality. We must know "when to hold them and when to fold them."

Go for your dreams! Make them happen! But be responsible!
Your mama and daddy can't raise you forever!

There are no limits to caring ®

January 4

*He has made everything beautiful in its time. He has also set
eternity in the human heart; yet no one can fathom what God has
done from beginning to end* (Ecclesiastes 3:11, NIV).

Time

"What time is it?" ... It's the first working week of a new year.
But really, what time is it? A new year! New opportunities.

We tend to think about time in terms of numbers. We count the
days. The ancient Greeks had a word for it ... *chronos*, from which
we get our word chronology.

The Greeks also had another word for time ... *Kairos*. *Kairos* had
to do with the content of time. What we do with time. It had to do
with opportunity.

We all have 24 hours in each day. The important thing is what we
do with those hours. Use your time today to reach out and offer a
helping hand or an encouraging word. That's a great way to begin
a new year!

Time is opportunity. Don't just count it, use it – to make our
community a better place.

There are no limits to caring ®

January 5

I press on toward the goal to win the prize for which God has called me heavenward in Christ Jesus. (Philippians 3:14, NIV).

Press On

Most of us are settled back into our regular schedules after the events of the holiday season. Some are relieved, and some are already anticipating next year's festivities.

Many have made resolutions for this year. I encourage you to continue pressing forward! If you stumble or get off track, that's ok. The important thing is that you continue to get back up, regroup, and keep working toward your goals.

Let this year be your best year yet! Focus on the positive in life and every situation and, no matter what comes your way, you can overcome!

Remember, we are not alone. The Bible says, "Greater is He that is in you than He that is in the world." That's great news! We are not working towards these resolutions and goals alone, but have help available. Press on...don't give up....

There are no limits to caring ®

January 6

Therefore, there is no condemnation for those who are in Christ Jesus
(Romans 8:1, NIV).

Can of Peas

An elderly woman was arrested for shop lifting in a supermarket. When she went before the judge he asked, "What did you steal from the store?" She told him that she had stolen a can of peaches.

The judge then asked her why she had stolen the can of peaches and she replied that she was hungry. The judge thought for a moment and then asked her, "How many peaches were in the can?"

She replied, "Six peaches were in the can." The judge said, "Then I will then give you 6 days in jail."

But before the judge could actually pronounce the punishment, the woman's husband stood up and asked the judge if he could say something.

The judge nodded and the husband said, "She also stole a can of peas."

We all made mistakes last year…but this new year, don't count the peas, look ahead to a fresh start, a clean slate.

There are no limits to caring ®

January 7

In all things I have shown you. . . we must help the weak and remember the words of the Lord Jesus, how he himself said, "It is more blessed to give than to receive" (Acts 20:35, ESV).

Dead Sea

In Israel, there is a body of water called the Dead Sea. It is called the Dead Sea because it only receives water and holds it. Nothing flows from it. The name is appropriate, for something that does not give is truly dead. We only find life when we learn to give.

There are basically two kinds of people: the takers and the givers. The takers may have more, but the givers sleep better at night. It is in the joy of giving where we find true life and true blessings. Your life can be a dead sea or it can be a sea of living water.

That is a choice each one of us will make every day. Reach out to those about you who have a need, to your family, your coworkers...you will be glad, and you will find life in the process.

There are no limits to caring ®

January 8

If any of you lacks wisdom, let him ask God, who gives
generously to all without reproach, and it will be given him
(James 1:5, ESV).

Try Something Different

Have you ever noticed a fly trying to escape, trying to fly through a closed window? There could be an open window, but the fly keeps on butting his head against the closed glass. His strategy is obvious: work harder.

However, with less energy, he could easily escape if only he would explore other options.

We often get so fixed on a way of life, that when it doesn't work, we try harder and harder, the same old way we've always done it.

What we really need is to stop butting our heads in the same old way—and look for new possibilities. Nothing changes - until something changes.

Trying harder may not be the solution to achieving more. Work smarter - not harder! Explore new possibilities when the old doesn't work any longer.

There are no limits to caring ®

January 9

Let each of you look not only to his own interests, but also to the interests
of others (Philippians 2:4, ESV).

Balance

A magnificent skyscraper was under construction. One day, as a metal beam was going up to be placed on the sixteenth floor, a workman leaned out to grab it. He lost his balance and began to fall. As he fell, he reached out and grabbed the steel beam. Desperately, he clung to the end of the beam. But the beam began to tilt, which would **cause** him to lose his grip and fall to his death.

Without hesitation, another worker on the same floor leaped into the air and landed on the other end of the beam. His weight caused the beam to level out and both men were safely lowered to the street.

Every day, people around us are losing their balance. It might be that single mother struggling to make ends meet, or the co-worker needing a word of encouragement … or your child.

Don't hesitate. Go out on a limb. Help someone keep their balance.

There are no limits to caring ®

January 10

Whatever your hand finds to do, do it with all your might...
(Ecclesiastes 9:10, NIV).

Expectations

Willie Nelson said, "I always do what I'm expected to do. Except when I don't." Can you identify?

Living up to expectations can be difficult. There are times when the expectations of others place a real burden on us because they are unrealistic. They expect us to do things we simply cannot do or behave in a manner not in keeping with our own personality.

And then there are times when we place unrealistic expectations on ourselves. Those can be the most demanding, leading to frustration. None of us can perform perfectly, because we are not perfect.

However, expectations are not all bad. They can motivate us to good behavior and better performance. We may not be perfect, but we can give our best efforts to whatever we do. We should always expect the best from ourselves regardless of what others may expect.

There are no limits to caring ®

January 11

I have told you these things, so that in me you may have peace. In this world you will have trouble. But take heart! I have overcome the world (John 16:33, NIV).

Life is a Journey

Have you heard the expression, "Life is a journey and I'm enjoying the ride?" Well, I think it's the *journey* that provides *Life*. We have all experienced hardships, challenges that push us to unexplored territory.

Maybe for you it's the death of a loved one, a serious illness, loss of job, divorce.

In these trials, we find depth of character that we may not have known we had. And we find there are those who have been there before us. And if we look around, we will see others who are in worse circumstances than our own.

Our life may take a different path than we imagined, but it just may be on those paths that we find a greater purpose for our journey. So, if your journey of life takes a different path than you thought, be open to opportunity. Look around and take that chance to make a difference.

There are no limits to caring ®

January 12

As iron sharpens iron, so one person sharpens another (Proverbs 27:17, NIV).

Overcome

Jack Chen had been athletic all his life, but since the age of sixteen, he had faced a significant challenge. He was blind. But he wasn't going to let that stop him. Rather than avoid the challenges caused by his blindness, he embraced them.

His goal was to become a triathlete and to compete in the Ironman competition. He worked with a coach who specifically assisted blind athletes. They would compete in the Ironman competition, tied together so that the coach could guide him and be his eyes.

Jack Chen swam, biked, and ran…covering several miles. He said he wanted to show the world that someone with impairments could do whatever they wanted. He won the competition in Panama City, which qualified him for the World Championship Ironman competition in Hawaii.

Surround yourself with supportive and encouraging people who can help you through the tough times.

There are no limits to caring ®

January 13

And let us not grow weary of doing good, for in due season we will reap, if we do not give up (Galatians 6:9, ESV).

Rejection

In 1962, four young musicians played their first record audition for the executives of a recording company. The executives were not impressed. When turning them down, one executive said, "We don't like their sound." The group was called The Beatles.

In 1944, the director of the Blue Book Modeling Agency told modeling hopeful Norma Jean Baker, "You better learn secretarial work or else get married." She went on to become Marilyn Monroe.

In 1954, the manager of the Grand Ole Opry fired a singer after one performance. He told him, "You ain't goin' nowhere son. You ought to go back to drivin' a truck." That singer was Elvis Presley.

It sometimes takes rejection for us to find our vision, become more ambitious, and ultimately achieve success. Champions do experience failures, but they succeed because they never quit.

There are no limits to caring ®

January 14

You will plant crops but not harvest them. You will press your
olives but not get enough oil to anoint yourselves. You will
trample the grapes but get no juice to make your wine (Micah
6:15, NLT).

Cheat

Emmanuel Nenger was at the grocery store. He handed the clerk a $20 bill for his purchase. As she took the money, she noticed that the ink from the $20 bill came off onto her fingers.

After Emmanuel left the store, the clerk called the police, suspecting him of giving the clerk counterfeit money.

The police arrived at the store and verified that it was a counterfeit bill. When they went to Emmanuel's home, they found that he had been painting $20 bills in his attic, displaying amazing artistic talent.

The police also found three portraits that Emmanuel had painted. They seized them and sold them at auction for $16,000 each. It took Emmanuel almost as long to paint one $20 bill as it did for him to paint a $16,000 portrait!

We cheat ourselves when we don't use our passions and talents for good. Be your best. The results are truly priceless.

There are no limits to caring ®

January 15

*And in the last days it shall be, God declares, that I will pour out
my Spirit on all flesh, and your sons and your daughters shall
prophesy, and your young men shall see visons, and your old men
shall dream dreams* (Acts 2:17, ESV).

M. L. King

I have a dream! . . ." With those words, Dr. Martin Luther King
spoke to the soul of our nation. His dream resonated in the hearts
of millions of people, and the social landscape of this country was
changed – for then and for decades to come, as millions of lives
were changed. You know, dreams are very powerful.

What are your dreams? Do you dream of a better day, a better
world, a better you? Dr. King had a dream of a better society. His
dream cost him everything. You too can see your dreams fulfilled,
but it will take total commitment to your dreams.

At VOA, we help people fulfill their dreams. You too can be a
dream maker. Make your dreams a reality.

There are no limits to caring ®

January 16

Dear friends, never take revenge. Leave that to the righteous anger of God... (Romans 12:19, NLT).

Revenge

B ill loved mystery theater. So, one evening, he took his wife Marie to a mystery theater show. They arrived late, and the usher took them to seats in the back, but they were too far from the stage.

Bill whispered to the usher, "This is supposed to be a good mystery show and I really want to sit closer. Get me a better seat, and I'll give you a handsome tip."

The usher agreed and took Bill and Marie to seats on the second row. Bill withdrew a quarter from his pocket and handed it to the usher.

The usher looked down at the quarter in his hand and then leaned over to Bill and whispered, "The maid did it, in the parlor, with the candlestick."

When people do you wrong, do you really want to be spiteful? At the end of the day, will revenge make you a happier person?

There are no limits to caring ®

January 17

Give thanks in all circumstances; for this is the will of God in Christ Jesus for you (1 Thessalonians 5:18, ESV).

Robert Louis Stevenson

Robert was always in poor health, and so he spent much of his time indoors, reading and writing short stories.

At 18, his father enrolled him in a university to pursue engineering. A few years later, he dropped out of school to pursue writing full time.

Robert traveled constantly in search of warmer climates that would improve his health. By traveling to locations such as Hawaii and Tahiti, he gathered inspirations and ideas to write some of his greatest novels, such as *Treasure Island* and *Dr. Jekyll and Mr. Hyde*.

Robert Louis Stevenson later wrote about his illness, saying, "I have so many things to be thankful for...it's a pity I can't have the one thing – health. But I believe...that it is for the best. I wouldn't change with any other man in my time."

We don't always know why we face difficult circumstances. But perhaps without them, we couldn't write the perfect story.

There are no limits to caring ®

January 18

A soft answer turns away wrath, but a harsh word stirs up anger
(Proverbs 15:1, ESV).

Eloped

A father passed by his daughter's bedroom and stopped when he saw a letter propped up on her pillow. It read:

Dad:

It is with great sorrow that I'm writing to you. I eloped with my boyfriend because I wanted to avoid a scene with you and Mom. I knew you wouldn't approve of Butch because of all his piercings, tattoos, and because he is so much older than I am.

I'm also pregnant. Butch and I are very happy. He owns a trailer in the woods and has a stack of firewood for the whole winter. Don't worry, I'll be 15 soon. Someday we'll be back to visit so you can meet your grandchildren.
Love, Mary

P.S. Dad, none of the above is true. I'm at Sara's house. I just wanted to remind you that there are worse things in life than my report card.

Children make mistakes. But we should never forget to affirm and acknowledge them when they do right.

January 19

Do not judge by appearances, but judge with right judgment
(John 7:24, ESV).

Assumptions

John was driving home late one night when he saw a hitchhiker along the road. Cautiously, he decided to stop and offer the hitchhiker a ride.

As they rode along, he began to be suspicious of his passenger. His coat was on the center console between them. John checked to see if his wallet was safe in the pocket of his coat, but it wasn't there!

So, he slammed on the brakes, turned to the hitchhiker and said, "Hand over the wallet immediately and get out of my car!"

The frightened hitchhiker handed over a wallet, jumped out of the car, and John drove off.

When he arrived home, he told his wife about the experience. As soon as he finished, his wife said, "John, did you know that you left your wallet at home this morning?"

Sometimes we jump to conclusions before we have all the facts. Don't jump so quickly. Know the facts before you judge.

There are no limits to caring ®

January 20

These men who have turned the world upside down have come here also (Acts 17:6, ESV).

Aim High

The greatest danger is not that we aim too high and miss the mark, but that our aim is too low, and we reach it. Robert Browning wrote, "Ah, but a man's reach should exceed his grasp or what's heaven for?"

Today, we can set our sight merely to get through the day – or we can set our sights to be great achievers – and the higher our goals, the greater our achievement.

God has entrusted opportunities to each of us. What we do with those opportunities has everything to do with stewardship. Aim high, and the stewardship will be greater; the people we bump into will be blessed, and our circle of influence will be greater than ever. Don't underestimate yourself – aim high and make a difference.

January 21

"Again, the kingdom of heaven is like a merchant looking for fine pearls. When he found one of great value, he went away and sold everything he had and bought it" (Matthew 13:45-46, NIV).

Irritation

What irritates you? A reckless driver? A crying child? A homeless person? Someone who is self-centered. What irritates you says much about your values.

Why is it when we get irritated we wind up with ulcers, and when oysters get irritated they wind up with pearls?

Maybe there are pearls that come out of your irritation. If you are irritated when you see a hungry man and you feed him, that's a pearl. If you are irritated when you see an elderly person mistreated, or ignored, and you befriend him, that's a pearl. If the sight of a neglected child irritates you, and you offer support and care, that's a pearl.

Just being irritated is not enough. It's what we produce as a result. When we make things better, we create pearls. We all have that opportunity to create pearls.

Which will it be for you today, ulcers or pearls? Go for the Pearls!

There are no limits to caring ®

January 22

The way of a fool is right in his own eyes, but a wise man listens to advice (Proverbs 12:15, ESV).

Dog Bite

Chris was very close to his black lab, Laney. That's why he was so surprised when he woke up to find her biting his foot, repeatedly.

Chris and two of his friends had been sleeping soundly in the basement over the Christmas break. They had planned to sleep late, but Laney had other plans. She started biting Chris' foot over and over and would not give up until he got out of bed.

So, Chris and his friends went upstairs to let Laney out and to eat breakfast. But as they went into the kitchen, smoke was everywhere. Apparently, the garage had caught fire sometime that morning and Laney, smelling the smoke, had awakened Chris.

Sometimes we want to sleep through unpleasant circumstances. But we all need a friend who can awaken us to reality. Trust the instincts of those who love you—even your dog—or it may come back to bite you in the foot.

January 23

But if serving the Lord seems undesirable to you, then choose for yourselves this day whom you will serve... but as for me and my household, we will serve the Lord (Joshua 24:15, NIV).

Reactions

We may not be responsible for everything that happens to us, but we are responsible for the way we react to those things. The best choice is to be positive.

- Choose to love rather than hate
- Choose to smile rather than frown
- Choose to build rather than destroy
- Choose to persevere rather than quit
- Choose to praise rather than gossip
- Choose to heal rather than wound
- Choose to laugh rather than cry
- Choose to give rather than take
- Choose to go rather than wait
- Choose to forgive rather than curse
- Choose to pray rather than despair

When we choose to respond negatively, we are only hurting ourselves. You ultimately choose your attitude. Make it positive. You'll be surprised how much better your day goes.

There are no limits to caring ®

January 24

Therefore, as God's chosen people, holy and dearly loved, clothe yourselves with compassion, kindness, humility, gentleness and patience (Colossians 3:12, NIV).

Babe Ruth

During his baseball career, Babe Ruth hit 714 home runs. But in one of his last games, he played very poorly. No longer as agile as he had once been, he made several errors, allowing the opponent to get ahead.

As he walked off the field and headed toward the dugout, the crowds began yelling and booing. Just then, a little boy jumped over the railing onto the playing field. With tears in his eyes, he ran up to Babe Ruth and hugged him.

Babe Ruth picked up the little boy, hugged him, and set him down on his feet, patting his head gently. A hush fell over the entire crowd.

The fans saw two heroes: Babe Ruth, who, despite his bad day on the field, still cared about a little boy; and the small boy, who cared about the feelings of another human being.

Be compassionate. You'll be surprised who needs your compassion.

January 25

So, teach us to number our days that we may get a heart of wisdom (Psalm 90:12, ESV).

The Bank

What if you had a bank account and each morning, your account would be credited with eighty-six thousand four hundred dollars. You could not carry over a balance, and every night the account deleted what you did not use. What would you do? Spend every cent, of course!

Each of us has such a bank – it's called time. Each morning, you are credited with eighty-six thousand four hundred seconds. Every night, you lose whatever time was not invested in a good purpose. You cannot carry over a balance, you can't borrow from tomorrow. If you fail to use the day's deposit, the loss is yours.

Invest your time wisely.
- Time invested in helping others
- Time invested in the welfare of your family
- Time invested on improving yourself

This is time well spent. The value of those investments will carry over again and again.

There are no limits to caring ®

January 26

If you have found honey, eat only enough for you, lest you have your fill of it and vomit it (Proverbs 25:16, ESV).

Pine Nuts

One evening at dinner, Molly ordered a salad with pine nuts. She discovered she loved the taste of pine nuts, so after dinner, she stopped by the store to purchase a large bag of pine nuts. The next day, she added the pine nuts to almost every dish she ate.

But over the next few days, everything she ate tasted bitter and metallic. Her husband said everything tasted fine, but Molly threw out food thinking it was bad. She brushed her teeth and used mouthwash. Still, the bitter taste was there.

It turns out that Molly had "pine nut mouth." It seems that if you eat pine nuts in excess, it can leave a metallic and bitter taste in your mouth for several days.

In everything in life, moderation is the key. Whether it's food, time, or even money. Too much of a good thing can leave a bad taste in your mouth.

January 27

Give to everyone who begs from you, and from one who takes away your goods do not demand them back (Luke 6:30, ESV).

Cookies

A lady went into the airport gift shop and bought a book and a bag of cookies. She took her seat in the waiting area and started reading her book.

From the corner of her eye, she saw the man sitting beside her open her bag of cookies. He reached in, took a cookie, and began eating it. She chose to ignore it to avoid a scene.

But every time she took a cookie, he would take one too. She couldn't believe how rude he was! He actually took the last cookie, broke it in half, and gave it to her!

Her flight was finally called, and she took her seat on the plane. She reached into her bag for her book, and lo and behold, there was her bag of cookies!

How many times have you eaten someone else's cookies and never known it?

There are no limits to caring ®

January 28

Bear one another's burdens, and so fulfill the law of Christ
(Galatians 6:2, ESV).

Load Lifting

A farm boy accidentally overturned his wagonload of corn. The farmer who lived nearby heard the noise and yelled to the boy, "Come over and have lunch, and I'll help you fix the wagon later."

"That's real nice of you," the boy replied, "but Paw wouldn't like it." "Come on over and have lunch," the farmer insisted. So, the boy agreed.

After lunch, the boy thanked his host and said, "I feel better now, but I know Paw is going to be real upset." "Don't be foolish," the farmer said. "By the way, where is your paw?" "Under the wagon!"

There are a lot of people in our community who are under a load. They need a hand up. It may be the young guy next door or the unemployed single parent down the street. You may have someone's name on your mind right now. Somewhere today you will bump into someone under a load. How about a hand up, now?

There are no limits to caring ®

January 29

The Lord detests lying lips, but he delights in people who are trustworthy (Proverbs 12:22, NIV).

Flat Tire

At an Ivy League university, there were four friends taking biology, and all of them had an "A" in the course. They were so confident in their grades that the weekend before final exams, they decided to visit some friends out of town and have a big party.

After all that hard partying, they didn't make it back to school until late Monday morning…just missing their final exam.

They agreed to tell their professor that they had a flat tire, which had caused them to be late and miss the exam.

The professor agreed to let them make up the final exam the next day. The friends were excited and relieved and studied all night for the exam.

The next day, the professor placed them in separate rooms and gave them a test booklet containing only one exam question. It asked, "For one hundred points, which tire was flat?"

Tell the truth – for that you'll always make a perfect score!

There are no limits to caring ®

January 30

So prepare your minds for action and exercise self-control...
(1 Peter 1:13, NLT).

Will Power

Vince Lombardi said, "The difference between a successful person and others is not a lack of strength, not a lack of knowledge, but rather a lack of will."

The real question to ask of ourselves as we approach any task is not, "Can I do it?" but, "Will I do it? Am I willing to invest the time and effort necessary to see the job through?"

Most of the jobs that are left unfinished or undone are not the result of a lack of skill, but rather a lack of will. People simply quit before they finish.

The key to success in any job or any relationship is the ability to persevere until the task is accomplished.

Whether it's a task at your workplace, building a home, or building a marriage, it is a matter of choice. "Will I complete what I have started?" Successful people answer that question with a "Yes!"

Will you finish what you start?

There are no limits to caring ®

January 31

The integrity of the upright guides them, but the crookedness of the treacherous destroys them (Proverbs 11:3, ESV).

New CEO

A CEO was preparing to retire and wanted to choose a successor. He gathered together all the executives in his company. He said, "I am giving each one of you a seed today. Bring them back one year from today. I will judge the plants that you bring and choose the next CEO."

Jim took his seed home and planted it. Every day, he watered it and cared for it. But months went by, and nothing ever grew.

A year passed, and it was time to bring the results in for inspection. The CEO inspected everyone's beautiful trees and plants. Suddenly, he spotted Jim's empty pot.

That's when he announced, "Meet your new CEO, Jim!" The CEO explained that the seeds he had distributed were dead and wouldn't grow. Jim had been the only one honest about his results.

Honesty always yields the best crop. What you plant now determines what you reap later.

There are no limits to caring ®

February 1

A joyful heart is good medicine, but a crushed spirit dries up the bones (Proverbs 17:22, ESV).

It's Chapped

Jake is a 4-year-old boy who loves Chapstick. He would always ask his mom if he could use her Chapstick. But then he would lose it. So, one day, his mom showed him where she kept her Chapstick...in her bathroom drawer. She explained that he could use it whenever he wanted, but he had to put it back when he finished.

One morning, Jake's mom couldn't find him anywhere. She looked all over the house and then found him in her bathroom.

To her horror, he was applying her Chapstick very carefully to the cat's rear end. Jake looked up at his mom and said, "It's chapped."

Now the important question is, was that the first time he had applied the Chapstick to the cat's rear end, or the fiftieth time?

Being a parent is always filled with questions – some things we'll never understand. Just do your best!

February 2

Jesus said, "Come." So, Peter got out of the boat and walked on water and came to Jesus (Matthew 14:29 **ESV**).

Optimist

A duck hunter bought a dog that could actually walk on water to retrieve a duck. Amazed by the dog, he was sure none of his friends would believe him.

He decided to take his friend, a pessimist by nature, to hunt with him and his new dog.

As they waited by the shore, a flock of ducks flew by. They fired, and a duck fell. The dog jumped into the water. But the dog did not sink! Instead, he walked across the water to retrieve the bird, never getting more than his paws wet.

The pessimist watched carefully but did not say a single word. On the drive home, the hunter asked his friend, "Did you notice anything unusual about my new dog?"

"I sure did," responded the pessimist. "He can't swim."

Today you can choose to see the good or the bad...be an optimist or a pessimist. What will your attitude be today?

There are no limits to caring ®

February 3

*I have labored and toiled and have often gone without
sleep. I have known hunger and thirst and have often gone
without food; I have been cold and naked*
(1 Corinthians 11:26-27, NIV).

Columbia

February 3, 2003, our country lost seven astronauts when the Columbia disintegrated 40 miles above the earth. They were pioneers. They went into the unknown and discovered what we did not know. Their families and colleagues still grieve because of what we lost.

That cool February morning, many people did not even know we had people heading out into space. We certainly were not expecting this disaster.

Perhaps if we've learned anything, we have learned that people place their lives in jeopardy every day—and most of the time we really don't think about it.

- Our policemen and firefighters, while we are asleep—doing whatever it takes to make our community safe.
- Our military that is all over the world and even here at home—protecting our freedom.

Are we willing to risk it all so that people in need might hear the Good News of Jesus Christ?

February 4

Cast all your anxiety on him because he cares for you (1 Peter 5:7, NIV).

Holding You Back

John decided to try out his new boat. But John was new to boating, and no matter how hard he tried, he couldn't get his boat to perform very well.

It was very sluggish and wouldn't steer correctly. So, John puttered into a nearby marina looking for someone there who could help him find out what was wrong with his boat.

A friendly boat captain offered to check John's boat for him. He checked it thoroughly...and found nothing wrong. So, he jumped into the water to look underneath the boat.

A few seconds later, he came up choking on water – he was laughing so hard. Under the boat, still strapped securely in place, was the trailer.

If you're not performing well, check to see what's holding you back. It may be something that you simply need to let go of so that the wind can fill your sail.

48

February 5

For there is nothing hidden that will not be disclosed, and nothing concealed that will not be known or brought out into the open (Luke 8:17, NIV).

Dishonesty Shows Up

One day, a mother sent her son to the post office to mail a letter. He came back with a suspicious smile on his face. "What happened?" the mother asked. "I just fooled the people at the post office. When no one was looking, I dropped the letter into the box without buying any stamps."

Needless to say, that letter didn't get off the ground and probably came right back to the mother. And the son was the only one fooled.

That's the way it works. Dishonesty doesn't get us off the ground and it always, sooner or later, comes right back to us. It's cheaper in the long run to be honest and ethical.

We live in a day and age when truth is whatever you want to make it, and we fail to recognize what is real. Be about honesty and ethical behavior; it will pay off, big time.

There are no limits to caring ®

February 6

Therefore, whenever we have the opportunity, we should do good to everyone—especially to those in the family of faith (Galatians 6:10, NLT).

Elvis Presley

Jimmy's friend played the guitar and needed someone to tune it for him. But Jimmy's parents didn't like his friend because he was from the wrong side of the tracks. They wouldn't even allow him in their home. So, Jimmy asked his uncle, country singer Lonzo Green, to tune his friend's guitar.

When Lonzo met Jimmy's friend, he noticed that the boy was self-conscious and obviously felt out of place in Lonzo's upscale neighborhood. Lonzo, who had also lived in poverty, was happy to tune the boy's guitar. He even taught him a few chords.

The boy thanked Lonzo and left with the warm memory of his kindness. Eventually that boy grew up, never to be poor again. We know him as the late Elvis Presley.

Your kindness, even to a boy from the wrong side of the tracks, will always be a blessing, even more than you can imagine.

There are no limits to caring ®

50

February 7

Therefore, knowing the fear of the Lord, we persuade others. But what we are is known to God, and I hope it is known also to your ***conscience***
(2 Corinthians 5:11, ESV).

Persuasion

A *Peanuts* comic strip a few years back has Sally saying to Linus, "I think I would be a good evangelist." "Why?" asks Linus. Sally answers, "I convinced the boy who sits behind me at school that my religion is better than his." "How did you do that?" asks Linus. Sally answers, "I hit him over the head with my lunch box."

There are obviously better ways to share your faith, convictions, and opinions. Sally's method will always fail to get another to truly agree with us, or to effect real change in another person.

Nothing can take the place of friendly persuasion. It's the old *honey versus vinegar* thing. Try serving up your opinions with a little "sweetness," and see if there aren't more takers!

February 8

Charm is deceptive, and beauty is fleeting; but a woman who fears the Lord is to be praised (Proverbs 31:30, NIV).

Beauty Tips

You can hardly watch television without seeing a commercial for a beauty product. Magazines are filled with beauty secrets and tricks. Walk down the aisle in a store and you'll be overwhelmed by the many beauty products.

But what are the real secrets to beauty – the ones that really work?

Audrey Hepburn wrote a poem when she was asked to share her "beauty tips." She wrote:

- For attractive lips, speak words of kindness.
- For lovely eyes, seek out the good in people.
- For a slim figure, share your food with the hungry.
- For beautiful hair, let a child run his/her fingers through it once a day.
- For poise, walk with the knowledge that you never walk alone. People, even more than things, have to be restored, renewed, revived, reclaimed, and redeemed; never throw anyone out.
- As you grow older, you will discover that you have two hands, one for helping yourself and the other for helping others.

Now, those "tips" will make each of us beautiful in our own way.

There are no limits to caring ®

February 9

-

Ask, and it will be given to you; seek, and you will find;
knock, and it will be opened to you (Matthew 7:7, ESV).

Sandbox

A little boy was playing in his sandbox. He had a box full of toy trucks and cars and a plastic shovel. As he dug down in the sand, he uncovered a large rock. He dug around it with his little shovel. He struggled hard to push the rock to the edge of the sandbox. Try as he may, he couldn't get it up over the edge of the box. In frustration, he burst into tears.

The boy's father was watching from the living room window. He walked to his son's side and asked, "Son, why didn't you use all the strength you had available?" The little fellow sobbed, "But I did, Daddy. I used everything I had!"

The father said, "No son, you didn't. You didn't ask me for help." The father then reached down and removed the rock.

Sometimes, help is closer than you think. It's available for the asking.

February 10

Let us examine our ways and test them, and let us return to
the Lord.
(Lamentations 3:40, NIV).

Reflection

A mother said to her son, "Go to your room and think about what you did today." He was not in real trouble, but she knew the importance of developing good character in her young boy by having him reflect on what he had done.

That's probably good advice for all of us. Go somewhere and reflect on what you have done today.

Have I been good? An available vessel for God to use?
Have I honored God with my time?
Have I honored my employer by working hard and being productive?
Was I able to let the love of God be shown through my actions?
Did I pay attention to people and treat them respectfully?
Am I grateful for the blessings God has given me today?

This is not a time to be critical of yourself, but simply to reflect on your day. What have I done today that makes a difference?

There are no limits to caring ®

February 11

Set your minds on things that are above, not on things that are on earth (Colossians 3:2, ESV).

What's Important

Two men were walking in Times Square. The air was filled with the noise of passing traffic, sirens screaming, horns honking, and tires squealing. Suddenly, one of the men said, "I hear a cricket." His friend thought he was crazy. He said, "There's no way you hear a cricket in all this noise." "No, I am certain," the friend said. He walked across the street, looked in some bushes, and sure enough, there was a cricket.

His friend was amazed. "You must have super hearing!" "No," he replied, "It all depends on what is important to you."

He then pulled some coins from his pocket and dropped them on the sidewalk. Even with all the noise, every head within twenty feet turned to see if the money was theirs. "See," the friend said. "What you hear all depends on what is important to you."

In our busy lives, we sometimes don't hear what's important. What's calling out to you?

There are no limits to caring ®

February 12

May he kiss me with the kisses of his mouth, for your expressions of affection are better than wine (Solomon 1:2, NASB).

Passion

An elderly couple was eating dinner when the husband asked his wife, "Do you remember the first time we kissed 50 years ago? We went behind the tavern where you leaned against the fence and I kissed you for the first time." She blushed and the husband smiled, "How about we go back there for old time's sake?"

So the elderly couple hobbled along, leaning on their walking sticks. Finally, they made their way behind the tavern to the fence. As they leaned against the fence, they suddenly erupted into the most furious passion.

A policeman, hearing the commotion, went to investigate and stood in amazement. They were making loud noises, moaning and screaming. Then they collapsed in exhaustion.

The policeman was amazed. He approached them saying, "That was something else. What's your secret?" Shaking, the old man replied, "Fifty years ago that wasn't an electric fence."

Don't let your marriage lose its spark. Keep the passion.

February 13

"Let all that you do be done in love (1 Corinthians 16:14, ESV).

Your Spouse

A young lady put an ad in a local paper that said, "Husband wanted." The next day she received over 100 letters, all with the same response, "Take my husband, please!"

Ready to trade in your husband or wife? It may be better to try to improve your existing relationship. The pasture may look greener on the other side but what really counts is what you do in your own back yard.

Marriage is a challenge. Someone said, "Marriage is the number one cause of divorce!" Yep. That's real smart.

The smart ones are those who learn who their mate is, reach out in love and compassion seeking to meet the needs of the other. Good marital relationships begin by being responsive to the needs of each other. Reach out to your spouse in a loving, caring way. Try it! Perhaps you will not feel like giving up on your wonderful mate.

There are no limits to caring ®

February 14

By this all people will know that you are my disciples, if you have love for one another (John 13:35, ESV).

I Love You

When they were married, they promised that by noon each day, they would have said three simple words to each other. Simple, but profound words. "I love you."

Over the years they never forgot that promise, and never failed to say before noon, "I love you." Sometimes a phone call, sometimes a note, but always before noon.

On Debbie's 50th birthday, as her husband backed down the driveway, she chased him down to say "I love you." Within a few hours, her husband was killed in a tragic automobile accident. The last words he heard from his wife, and the last words she said to him, were simply "I love you." Their promise was never broken.

Don't forget to tell your spouse, your children, your parents, "I love you." It may be your last chance. There are no limits to caring for your family.

There are no limits to caring ®

February 15

Commit to the Lord whatever you do, and he will establish your plans. (Proverbs 16:3, NIV).

Pursue Your Goals

In 1954, medical experts said that the human body couldn't run a four-minute mile...the body was just not able to withstand that much pressure.

But a young medical student, Roger Bannister, ran a mile in under four minutes. And today, competitors routinely run a mile in less than four minutes.

In the early 1900's, experts said that high jumpers would never be able to jump over 7 feet. Then a man named Fosbury discovered that high jumpers were jumping the wrong way over the bar; instead of going feet first, they should go over headfirst and backward.

Everyone ridiculed him while he worked on this unorthodox way to jump over the high bar. Critics called it "the Fosbury Flop." But, he jumped over 7 feet! People may say...you can't do that! But, just maybe, you can. Don't let your dreams flop. To give up is to fail.

There are no limits to caring ®

February 16

Do to others as you would have them do to you (Luke 6:31, NIV).

Wooden Bowl

A frail old man went to live with his son, daughter-in-law, and their four-year-old son. The old man's hands shook so badly that he constantly dropped his food, spilled his drink, and created a real mess at mealtime.

His son and daughter-in-law became so irritated that they made him sit at a small table by himself and eat out of a large wooden bowl. They scolded him each time he dropped something. The four-year-old son didn't miss any of this.

One day, the little boy was working with some wood scraps on the floor. The father asked what he was building, and the boy replied, "I'm making some wooden bowls for you and Mom to eat out of when you get old."

The truth is, the way we treat our parents influences the way our children treat us. Compassionate care always comes home.

There are no limits to caring ®

February 17

Better the poor whose walk is blameless than a fool whose lips are perverse (Proverbs 19:1, NIV).

Honesty

During the political career of Abraham Lincoln, he was given the nickname *Honest Abe*. He earned it the old-fashion way - by being forthright and by being truthful in his dealings with people. It was a mark of integrity, of character.

Being honest should be simple. You either cheated or you didn't cheat on a test, which was it? However, as simple as it may seem in our modern world, truth seems so complex. And difficult to tell.

Jesus said, "You shall know the truth, and the truth will make you free," He did not say it would be easy, but he did say that truth would produce the best of all results. If we want the best for our lives, then honesty is still the best policy.

There are no limits to caring ®

February 18

You do not have because you do not ask God (James 4:3, NIV).

Unlikely Help

A woman was running errands one evening, only to find that she had locked her keys in her car.

She asked the Lord to send someone to help her. Just then, a rough-looking biker pulled up to her car. He was dressed in leather, with tattoos all over his arms.

The biker got off his motorcycle and approached her, asking if she needed any help. Hesitantly, she explained that she'd locked her keys in her car.

He returned to his bike and pulled out some tools from his bag. And within 60 seconds, he unlocked her car. The woman threw her arms around him and thanked him for his help.

Then the biker said, "Ma'am, don't thank me; I just got out of prison for stealing cars." She laughed and replied, "Well, I asked God for help, and He sent a professional."

You never know in what form help will arrive. Don't be so quick to judge or you may find yourself stranded.

There are no limits to caring ®

February 19

*Therefore, we do not lose heart. Though outwardly we are
wasting away, yet inwardly we are being renewed day by
day. For our light and momentary troubles are achieving for us
an eternal glory that far outweighs
them all* (2 Corinthians 4:16-17, NIV).

Deep Roots

Dr. Gibbs was a physician. When he wasn't saving lives, he was planting trees. He had a passion for gardening. His home sat on several acres of land, and his goal was to fill every acre with trees.

But he took a very unconventional approach to growing his trees. He never watered them.

He believed that watering the trees would make their roots grow shallow. If they weren't watered, they had to grow deep roots to find the moisture they needed to survive. This made them stronger, and they were then able to stand up to the strongest winds.

In the same way, we would rather not endure hardships (or grow deep roots), but life is full of storms. And we will always encounter those difficult times. But difficult times are what enable us to grow deep roots and to be stronger. Then we can stand tall – even when the winds would uproot us.

There are no limits to caring ®

February 20

To all who mourn… he will give a crown of beauty for ashes, a joyous blessing instead of mourning, festive praise instead of despair. In their righteousness, they will be like great oaks that the LORD has planted for his own glory (Isaiah 61:3, NLT).

Volcanoes

The volcanic eruption in Iceland in 2010 was devastating to many, and at the least, it interrupted the lives of millions of people. When a volcano erupts, it is terrifying and devastating.

But, out of the devastation, good things emerged. For example,
- Soon after the lava cooled, plants began to grow again.
- The hardened lava became rock and was used by builders.
- The lava rocks could be used for water filtration.
- Nutrients enriched the soil.
- Shorelines were expanded.
- Underwater volcanoes also can create new islands and habitats.

We can see God's redemptive hand at work, even through such devastation.

Many of us have also experienced devastation and pain. Hang on! The hand of God is at work, even in your life… though in the midst of chaos, it can be difficult to see His hand.

But God can take your situation and create something beautiful. Just like Isaiah said, "God can make beauty from ashes."

There are no limits to caring ®

February 21

Have I not commanded you? Be strong and courageous. Do not be frightened, and do not be dismayed, for the Lord your God is with youwherever you go
(Joshua 1:9, ESV).

Courage

One morning, Ray was working in his backyard which was bordered by a rain-flooded creek.

Suddenly, he saw a small girl being swept along the flooded creek. Without thinking, Ray ran and leapt into the rushing water. He was able to grab the little girl and, with his other hand, grab onto a limb protruding from the bank. He clung desperately to the branch, hoping help would arrive soon.

But by the time rescuers arrived, Ray had pulled the girl to safety. Ray was awarded the Coast Guard's Silver Lifesaving Medal, not only for selflessly rescuing the little girl, but because he was at a greater risk than people knew. Ray Blankenship couldn't swim!

Courage...what about your life, what courage is required? Mark Twain said, "Courage is...mastery of fear...not absence of fear." Control your fear; be courageous.

February 22

Love bears all things, believes all things, hopes all things,
endures all things (1 Corinthians 13:7, ESV).

George Washington

In October 1789, George Washington prepared to have his picture painted for Mrs. Washington. He combed his hair and put on the blue uniform he had worn as Commander of the Continental Army. He set off to meet his artist.

Sitting for two hours for the miniature painting was no fun for Washington; he hated it. However, he wanted to give a love gift to his wife. This picture was placed in a locket and worn with love by Mrs. Washington. Over a decade ago, it brought $900,000.

Washington endured discomfort for two hours to create a picture that his wife wore with love. Today, it has a great price tag.

Those "little things" you do for your mate will grow in value; the sacrifices you make will live on for generations to come. Find a way to express your love—love that will last a lifetime.

There are no limits to caring ®

66

February 23

*Now to him who is able to do far more abundantly than all that
we **ask or think, according to the power at work within us.**
(Ephesians 3:20, ESV)*

Bigger Frying Pan

Two friends, Tom and Joe, went fishing one morning. Tom was
an experienced fisherman; Joe wasn't. Every time that Tom
caught a big fish, he put it in his ice chest to keep it fresh; whenever
Joe caught a big fish, he threw it back.

After watching this go on all day, Tom finally asked, "Why do you
keep throwing back all the big fish?" Joe replied, "My frying pan
is not big enough for those big fish."

We laugh at Joe, who didn't realize that all he needed was a bigger
frying pan. Sometimes, like Joe, we throw back the big plans, big
dreams, big hopes, or even big opportunities that come our way
because our faith in ourselves is not big enough. We settle for less.

Now tell me, is your frying pan big enough for the opportunities
that will come to you today? With God's help, you won't have to
throw back the big fish.

There are no limits to caring ®

February 24

*I lift up my eyes to you, to you who sit enthroned in
heaven* (Psalm 123:1, NIV).

Look Up

If you put a buzzard in a box eight feet square and entirely open at the top, he will never be able to escape. The reason is that a buzzard always begins a flight from the ground by running. Without space to run, he will not even attempt to fly. He will remain a prisoner for life in a topless box.

Bats, likewise, are unable to fly if they are on a flat place. They have to throw themselves into the air from some elevation.

Bumblebees, if dropped into an open container, will die because they never look up.

Sometimes we are like buzzards, bats, and bumblebees. We struggle in our box of hopelessness without looking up.

There is always a solution to our problems if we but reach out. It may be a friend, a family member, or the Good Lord above. Look up! You'll be glad you did.

There are no limits to caring ®

February 25

Therefore, encourage one another and build one another up, just as you are doing (1 Thessalonians 5:11, ESV).

In Your Corner

D an Rather loved the sport of boxing. He played in high school, even though he admitted that he was never good at it.

But he learned a great deal from his coach, who taught the team what it meant to be a "get up again" fighter.

Dan Rather explained that a boxer is in a ring, completely on his own. And an experience that he will never forget is when he gets knocked down but then gets back up again. It gives the boxer a sense of achievement.

And sometimes, the only thing that drives a boxer to get up again is having someone in his corner of the ring, cheering for him.

In life, we all get knocked down now and then. We all need someone in our corner, to help us roll with the punches. And we all need to be in someone's corner, cheering for them. Be an encourager, help someone get up again.

There are no limits to caring ®

February 26

*Come to me, all you who are weary and burdened, and I will give
you rest* (Matthew 11:28, NIV).

Run Away

During difficult times, do you ever just want to run away?
When my son Josh was six, he announced to me that he was
going to run away and then quickly said, "Do you want to come
with me?"

All of us, in some form or another, are affected by an economic
meltdown…loss of job, loss of retirement.

How do we handle these challenging times?
- First, face head on the challenge that confronts you…don't
  run.
- Second, be gracious to one another. People all around us
  have an unusual amount of stress.
- Third, be kind…everyone needs kindness, now more than
  ever.
- Fourth, find ways to restore yourself…daily.
- Fifth, find ways to escape, but for a brief period of time.

Maybe that's what my six-year-old son was really saying – "I need
a break, will you go with me." Jesus said, "Come unto me and I
will give you rest."

There are no limits to caring ®

February 27

There is no fear in love. But perfect love drives out fear (1 John 4:18, NIV).

Brakes

Two riders were on a two-man bicycle when they came to a steep hill. They both agreed to continue up the hill. The climb was difficult, and they struggled to ascend the steep hill. After a terrific amount of effort, they finally made it to the top.

The front man, sweating profusely and breathing hard, turned back to his companion to say, "Boy, that sure was a hard climb."

The other guy responded, "It sure was, and if I had not kept the brakes on, we would have certainly rolled back down the hill."

Some want to make it to the top. Others just want to keep from going backwards.

I want to go to the top. I don't want to live in fear of going backwards.

Like in a marriage, in our jobs, in ALL of our relationships, we have to pedal together at the same time if we want to move forward.

Don't brake when you need to be pedaling!!

There are no limits to caring ®

February 28

For we are his workmanship, created in Christ Jesus for good works, which God prepared beforehand, that we should walk in them (Ephesians 2:10, ESV).

The Parable of the Pencil

A Pencil Maker took a pencil aside and said **to the pencil**, "There are 5 things you must know to be a great pencil.

~ "One: You'll do great things, but only if you allow yourself to be held in someone's hand.
~ "Two: You'll experience a painful sharpening sometimes, but you'll need it to become better.
~ "Three: You are able to correct mistakes you make.
~ "Four: The most important part of you will always be what's inside.
~ "And Five: On every surface you are used, you must leave your mark."

So it is with us. We will do great things if we allow ourselves to be in God's hand. We may experience pain sometimes, but it will make us stronger people. We have the power to correct our mistakes. What's most important is what is inside us.

And finally, as we will leave our mark no matter the situation, do what is right.

There are no limits to caring ®

March 1

Behold, I am doing a new thing; now it springs forth, do you not perceive it?I will make a way in the wilderness and rivers in the desert (Isaiah 43:19, ESV).

Find A Better Way

One evening Sara was helping her mom prepare a roast for dinner when she saw her mother cut the end of the roast off. Sara asked her mother why she did this. "Well, my mother always cut the end of the roast off and her mother did, and her mother before that too."

Being an inquisitive child, Sara went to the phone to call her grandmother…who didn't know why, only that her mother had cut the end of the roast off and her mother before that too.

So, Sara called other family members and finally found someone who knew the origins of the strange way to prepare a roast.

Her great aunt laughed as she told Sara that it began when her grandmother had to cut the end of the roast off because it was too big for her pan.

In our difficult times, we must find better ways to get the job done. The way we have always done it may not work. Find a better way.

March 2

*He reached down from on high and took hold of me; he drew me
out of deep waters. He has rescued me from my powerful enemy,
from my foes, who were too strong for me*
(Psalms 18:16-17, NIV).

Stuck in the Muck

In Florida, a man training for a marathon went running during his
lunch hour. But he never returned to his office. His friends and
co-workers soon became worried and sent out search parties to look
for him.

Four days later, his friends finally found him. He had spent the last
four days stuck in a mucky swamp up to his waist. The thick mud
acted like glue and would not let him go.

With only swamp water to drink, he was very thirsty and covered
with bug bites, but was otherwise okay.

In the muck of life, we sometimes get stuck and need someone to
help us out. It may be those bills that keep piling up with no relief
in sight. Or it may be the pain of losing a loved one, or it could be
depression.

Whatever it is, someone is reaching out to help you…will you take
their hand? Reach out and let someone help you out of the
muckiness of life.

There are no limits to caring ®

March 3

Rejoice with those who rejoice, weep with those who weep
(Romans 12:15, ESV).

Cab Driver

Late one night, a cab driver responded to a call. Upon reaching his destination, a frail, elderly woman appeared, dragging a suitcase behind her. Inside the cab, she gave an address and asked to go the long way around. "I'm in no hurry," said the woman. "I'm on my way to a hospice. The doctor says I don't have very long to live."

Quietly, the driver shut off the meter. For two hours, they drove around the city to several places from her past. She shared many fond memories along the way. Finally, reaching the hospice, she asked how much she owed. "Nothing," said the driver as he gave her a hug. She held him tightly and said, "You gave an old woman a moment of joy. Thank you."

The driver realized that he had never done anything more important in his life. People may not remember what you said, but they will always remember how they felt.

There are no limits to caring ®

March 4

But thanks be to God! He gives us the victory through our Lord Jesus Christ (1 Corinthians 15:57, NIV).

Shark

Jim is a 68-year-old man who is still able to pursue his passion of surfing. One day he was surfing off a Hawaiian beach when he suddenly felt something thump his surfboard.

He looked down and was horrified to see that a large shark was taking a bite out of his board. The shark continued to attack the surfboard, and Jim realized the situation was very dangerous. His surfboard would soon be useless.

So, he did the unthinkable. He grabbed the shark's fin, pulling himself onto its back, straddling it. Then he held on tightly and rode the shark.

When the shark became preoccupied with the surfboard, Jim slipped off its back and quickly swam to shore.

Life will always bring you challenges that threaten to sink you. You're never too old to take control of your situation. Is your attitude one of defeat or victory? Your choice…come out on top.

There are no limits to caring ®

March 5

I will refresh the weary and satisfy the faint (Jeremiah 31:25, NIV).

Loosen the Bow

In Athens, long ago, a man once saw the great storyteller Aesop playing games with little children. The man laughed, asking him why he wasted time in such a silly activity.

Aesop responded by picking up a hunting bow and loosening the string so that it was no longer stretched tight. Then he asked the man a riddle. "What does the unstrung bow imply?"

The man looked at the hunting bow for several moments but had no idea what point Aesop was trying to make. Aesop explained, "If you keep a bow always bent, it will break eventually; but if you let it go slack, it will be more fit for use when you want it."

People are also like that. That's why we all need to take time to rest. Set aside a special time to relax physically and renew yourself emotionally and spiritually. You're at your best when you take time to loosen up.

There are no limits to caring ®

March 6

*This is the day that the LORD has made; let us rejoice and
be glad in it* (Psalms 118:24, ESV).

Postpone Happiness

When can you choose to be happy? Some people postpone being happy, believing happiness will come after some event takes place.
- after the wedding
- after graduation
- after getting your driver's license
- after the right person comes along
- after the wrong person leaves
- after the stock market comes back
- after the kids leave home
- after you lose ten pounds
- after you gain ten pounds
- after you get the right job
- after you retire.

If you have to check everything off your list before you can choose to be happy, you will never make it. People who postpone happiness will never find it. Happiness is a journey, not a destination. The only time for happiness is now. Happiness is a byproduct - when we realize every moment of life is a gift and a gift to be shared.

Treasure this day and choose to be happy now.

There are no limits to caring ®

March 7

If you don't do what you know is right, you have sinned (James 4:17, CEV).

Might and Right

In our world, it seems a lot of times "the big dog always gets the bone." However, there is a timeless moral truth: Might... does not make right. While it is true that those exercising the greatest power seem to usually get their way, there is such a thing as moral authority.

Power is the ability to control things; moral authority is the ability to change things. While the majority may be satisfied with having things controlled, some people opt for moral authority and change our world for the better.

Pharaoh had power, but Moses had moral authority. Pilate had power, but Jesus had moral authority.

Doing the right thing and having moral authority, while also (always) holding the power may be harder and take longer, but remember... right is better than might. Just do the right thing.

There are no limits to caring ®

March 8

Give justice to the weak and the fatherless; maintain the right of the afflicted and the destitute. Rescue the weak and the needy; deliver them from the hand of the wicked (Psalms 82:3-4, ESV).

VOA Birthday

On March 8, 1896, Volunteers of America was founded by the Christian social reformers Maud and Ballington Booth. The organization was dedicated to "reaching and uplifting" all people.

The Booths envisioned reaching out to the needy and demonstrating the love of God to them. They offered other people a way to live out their faith. Their vision continues to live because they dared to dream of how to make their world a better place.

On this day, hundreds of thousands of lives are touched by a vision that began over a century ago, by a man and woman who said, "Whatever it takes, we can do it." There are no limits to caring. You can be a part of that network of caring people.

There are no limits to caring ®

March 9

In their hearts, humans plan their course, but the Lord establishes their steps (Proverbs 16:9, NIV).

Lost Sailor

An old sailor constantly got lost at sea, so his friends gave him a compass to use. The next time he went out in his boat, he followed their advice and took the compass with him. But, as usual, he got lost.

Finally, he was rescued by his friends. They were frustrated with him and asked, "Why didn't you use that compass we gave you? You could have saved us a lot of trouble!"

The sailor explained, "Well, I wanted to go north, but as hard as I tried to make the needle point in that direction, it kept on pointing south."

The sailor had stubbornly tried to force his compass to point him in the direction he wanted to go. Unable to do so, he had tossed the compass overboard.

Sometimes we stubbornly think we know the direction to go. But we all need a compass for direction in our lives. Where is your compass, and what do you do with it?

March 10

But he said to me, "My grace is sufficient for you, for my power is made perfect in weakness." Therefore, I will boast all the more gladly of my weaknesses, so that the power of Christ may rest upon me. For the sake of Christ, then, I am content with weaknesses, insults, hardships, persecutions, and calamities. For when I am weak, then I am strong (2 Corinthians 12:9-10, ESV).

Weakness to Strength

Sometimes your biggest weakness becomes your biggest strength. A small boy decided to study judo. He had no left arm. His teacher taught him only one move, saying, "This is the only move you will need."

At the boy's first tournament, he continued to win. In the finals, the opponent was bigger, stronger, more experienced. Finally, his opponent made a critical mistake. The boy used his one move to pin him, and he became the champion!

Afterwards, the boy asked his teacher, "How did I win the tournament with only one move?" The teacher answered, "You won for two reasons. First, you've mastered one of the most difficult throws in all of judo. Second, the only known defense for that move is for your opponent to grab your left arm."

The boy's biggest weakness became his biggest strength.

There are no limits to caring ®

March 11

And now these three remain: faith, hope and love. But the greatest of these is love
(1 Corinthians 13:13, NIV).

Love My Dog

Rob Gilbert tells of seeing a man walking a dog who was wearing shoes. The dog, that is. Wearing shoes. Gilbert was so taken by the sight, he asked the man why the dog was wearing shoes.

The dog's owner said, "My dog is so old that he has worn all the padding off his paws, and without the protective shoes, it would be like walking on hot coals. My dog is 15 ½ years old, and I have had him since he was a pup."

Gilbert gushed, "That's amazing. What's your secret? You should write a book about caring for dogs." The man responded, "It would be a very short book because I have only one secret." "What's that?" Gilbert asked. He said, "I really love my dog."

And that's also the secret to any relationship – to our spouse, our children, our friends.

There are no limits to caring. Even for your dog.

There are no limits to caring ®

March 12

*But we were gentle among you, like a nursing mother taking care
of her own children* (1 Thessalonians 2:7, ESV).

Substitute Parents

Traveling across the country, a 6-year-old girl was flying alone.
The airline steward told the lady seated next to the girl that the
young girl was alone and missing her mother.

Fortunately, the lady proved to be a very loving, nurturing person
who in effect became a substitute mother during the 3½ hour flight.
She provided comfort and security to a little girl who was lonely
and afraid.

As adults we will bump into little boys and little girls along life's
way who are flying solo…who may need a substitute parent…for
just a moment, a day, or even a lifetime.

All children are entitled to be loved and nurtured. It may be a
lonely 6-year-old flying across the country. It may be the child of
a single parent down the street. Look around. When you see the
children, you may find your opportunity to be a substitute parent.

There are no limits to caring ®

March 13

*But to all who did receive him, who believed in his name, he gave
the right to become children of God* (John 1:12, ESV).

Who's Your Daddy?

A single mother was raising her son in Tennessee. The young boy was often asked, "Who is your daddy?" "I don't have a daddy," he would reply. When the boy was about twelve years old, a new preacher came to his church. The boy tried to slip out early to avoid the question, but the preacher stopped and asked him, "Who is your daddy?" The whole church became silent. The preacher said, "I know who you are...you are a child of God. You've got a great inheritance. Go and claim it!"

From that moment on, when he was asked the question, "Who's your daddy," the boy would always say, "I'm a child of God."

If that preacher had not told him he was one of God's children, he would have never amounted to anything. This child of God is Ben Hooper, former governor of Tennessee.

As a child of God, go forth and claim your inheritance.

March 14

No one should seek their own good, but the good of others
(1 Corinthians 10:24, NIV).

Good Seeds

An aggressive and ambitious farmer was not satisfied with the yield of his corn crops. He heard about a highly recommended new corn seed. So, he bought new corn seeds. At the end of the harvest, the new seed had produced a crop that was so abundant his neighbors were amazed.

They asked the farmer to sell them a portion of the new seed. But the competitive farmer was afraid that he would lose his profit. He refused to sell.

The second year, the new seed did not produce as good a crop, and the third-year crop was even worse. The farmer soon found that his prize corn was being pollinated by the inferior grade corn from his neighbors' fields.

When we look out only for self, we don't produce the best. When we try to have it all, we often end up with nothing. We need to work together. That always produces the best results.

March 15

There is a way that appears to be right, but in the end, it leads to death (Proverbs 14:12, NIV).

Change Course

A battleship was training at sea in heavy weather for several days. The visibility was poor with patchy fog, so the commanding officer remained on the bridge keeping an eye on all activities.

Shortly after dark, the lookout on the wing of the bridge reported a light heading in their direction. It was on a dangerous collision course with their ship.

The commanding officer shouted to his men, "Signal the ship! Tell them we are on a collision course. Advise them to change course." Back came a reply, "Advisable for you to change course!"

The officer was furious and replied, "This is a battleship. Change course now!"

Back came the flashing light's reply. "This is a lighthouse! You'd better change course!" The battleship did change course.

Knowing when to change the course and when to stay the course is not always that clear! Evaluate where you're headed. Know when to change the course and when to stay the course.

There are no limits to caring ®

March 16

The point is this: whoever sows sparingly will also reap sparingly, and whoever sows bountifully will also reap bountifully (2 Corinthians 9:6, ESV).

Echo

A father and son were walking in the mountains. Suddenly the son fell. Hurting himself he screamed:"AAhhhhhhhhhhh!!!"

To his surprise, a voice repeated: "AAhhhhhhhhhh!!!" Curious, he yelled: "Who are you?" He received the answer: "Who are you?" Becoming angry, he screamed: "Coward!" In return, he heard: "Coward!"

He looked to his father and asked: "What's going on?" The father smiled and said: "My son, pay attention." And the father screamed: "I admire you!"

The voice answered: "I admire you!" Again he screamed: "You are a champion!"

The voice answered: "You are a champion!"

But the boy didn't understand. The father explained: "People call this an ECHO, but really this is LIFE. It gives you back everything you say or do. Our life is simply a reflection of our actions."

If you want more love and kindness, give more love and kindness. What you do has a way of coming back like an echo.

There are no limits to caring ®

March 17

The kingdom of heaven is like a grain of mustard seed .... It is the
smallest of all seeds, but when it has grown it is larger than all
the garden plants and becomes a tree, so that the birds of the air
come and make nests in its branches
(Matthew 13:31-32, ESV).

The Wright Brothers

Over a hundred years ago, Orville and Wilbur Wright made the first flight. They achieved what some thought was impossible. With very limited resources, they reached beyond the limitations of their time.

It wasn't easy. They failed along the way. But after each failure, they were motivated to work harder. They never gave up.

The Wright Brothers laid the foundation for other great accomplishments, such as Charles Lindbergh's first non-stop flight from New York to Paris; and Amelia Earnhardt's feat of being the first woman to fly solo across the Atlantic.

The Wright Brothers probably would not believe that the distance they flew is less than the distance between the wingtips of a 747 airplane. A short flight, but a huge achievement.

Sometimes we do things that seem small ...we just never know how someone else will build upon what we do. Be your best. And just do it, the rest will come in time.

There are no limits to caring ®

March 18

*Jesus said, "Let the little children come to me, and do not hinder
them, for the kingdom of heaven belongs to such as these"*
(Matthew 19:14, NIV).

Worms

A minister used a visual demonstration during his Sunday sermon. At the beginning of his sermon, he took four worms and placed them into four separate jars.

The first worm was put into a jar containing alcohol. In a few minutes, the worm was dead. The second worm was put into a jar filled with cigarette smoke…and it died shortly after.

The third worm was put into a jar of chocolate syrup. It too died. The fourth worm was put into a jar of good, clean soil. However, this worm did not die. Before making his conclusion, the minister turned and asked the congregation what they learned.

A young boy in the back raised his hand and said, "As long as you drink, smoke and eat chocolate, you won't have worms."

Children are our future and need to be taught well. They are watching everything we do and say…make sure you are living a good example.

There are no limits to caring ®

March 19

Those who are kind benefit themselves (Proverbs 11:17, NIV).

One Man's Treasure

Ernie Harris worked for 30 years as a valet at Chicago's exclusive Hawthorne House Apartments. He knew every resident by name. Every day he gave them a cheery greeting.

Everywhere he went, Ernie always carried two large overstuffed shopping bags. Some people speculated that Ernie was a closet millionaire and those bags held his fortune.

The mystery was solved after Ernie was tragically killed on his way to work. The residents turned their lobby into a shrine filled with flowers in tribute to their beloved Ernie.

Meeting his wife for the first time, they asked, "What did he carry in those bags?" It turned out the bags did carry his treasure. They were filled with 30 years' worth of cards and letters from residents expressing appreciation to Ernie for brightening their day.

Ernie was rich in the investment earned from a lifetime of kindness.

There are no limits to caring ®

March 20

Forget what happened long ago! Don't think about the past. I am creating something new (Isaiah 43:18-19, CEV).

Oscar

One day Oscar was fishing in the Caribbean. He'd never caught so many fish in his life. Every time he put his hook in the water, he pulled up a big beautiful redfish. This was the best fishing that he had ever done. It was so good that he wanted to be able to come back.

So, he took a big marker and marked the spot.... but he marked it in the bottom of the boat! A GPS system might have been better for Oscar. Obviously, Oscar never made it back to that spot.

We can never really go back to where we were because the spot is never in the same place. In difficult times like we're in now, we long for the good ole days, the great spots of life, but even today's times have the potential of good.

Every spot is changing. We must learn to fish here and now, not in the places we were.

There are no limits to caring ®

March 21

Whatever you do, work heartily, as for the Lord and not for men (Colossians 3:23, ESV).

House Builder

Ray had been building houses for 25 years. He came to his boss and said, "I'm ready to retire. I have worked hard for 25 years, and I need to retire and enjoy life." His boss agreed and said, "I have one last house for you to build." Reluctantly, he agreed to build one last house.

As he built the last house, he skipped a few nails here and there, cut a few corners, didn't put his usual quality into the house—after all, he was retiring.

Finally, the house was complete. Ray gave the keys to his boss and said, "Here are the keys. I've finished the house." His boss said, "No, Ray, you keep the keys. This house is a gift from me to you for all the years of hard work."

Each day we are building our life. We get out of life what we put into it.

March 22

*Do not conform to the pattern of this world, but be transformed
by the renewing of your mind* (Romans 12:2, NIV).

Butterfly

The butterfly is an interesting insect. We could learn a lot from it. But the colorful and beautiful butterfly was not always lovely.

On its journey to change from a worm to a butterfly, it must first go through metamorphosis. This process takes time. After all, change doesn't happen overnight.

And before that butterfly can emerge from its protective cocoon, it has to struggle to get out of that cocoon. Straining and persisting. If someone were to crack the cocoon open and release the butterfly, it would be unable to fly. It is the struggle to emerge from the cocoon that gives the butterfly strength to survive and fly.

And just like the butterfly, we often experience difficulties on the journey to change. Through difficulties we learn, grow, and become more of what God intended us to be…beautiful.

There are no limits to caring ®

March 23

A friend loves at all times, and a brother is born for a time of adversity (Proverbs 17:17, NIV).

Support

Three-year-old Kyndall loves princesses. One afternoon, her father brought her a set of princess figurines. And each princess also came with a friend: one was a fish, another was a tiger, and another was a teapot.

As Kyndall played with the figurines, she became frustrated trying to get each princess to stand up. They kept falling over.

So, her father placed each princess next to her friend, so that each princess figurine leaned on a friend. And the figurines were able to stand up.

Kyndall was delighted. "They stand better with their friends, Daddy!"

No matter how pretty you are, everyone needs a friend. We stand better and taller in the company of our friends and family.

Maybe you are going through a difficult time right now. Whatever the situation, stand together. You're always stronger.

There are no limits to caring ®

March 24

*So we fix our eyes not on what is seen, but on what is unseen,
since what is seen is temporary, but what is unseen is eternal* (2
Corinthians 4:18, NIV).

The View

The story is told of two men, both aged and seriously ill,
occupying the same hospital room. They talked for hours,
sharing their life stories.

One man managed to sit up in his bed for an hour each afternoon
looking out the room's only window. He would describe the
beautiful landscape. A lake with graceful swans. Grand old trees.
One day, he described a parade passing by.

After several days, the man by the window died. The other man
asked the nurse to be moved by the window so he could see the
view. When he was finally able to look out the window, all he could
see was a brick wall across the street.

He asked the nurse how his roommate was able to describe such
wonderful things outside the window. She said, "You know, he was
blind. What he saw came from within."

Circumstances need not control how we see life.

There are no limits to caring ®

March 25

*Do nothing from selfish ambition or conceit, but in humility count
others more significant than yourselves. Let each of you look not
only to his own interests, but also, to the interests of others*
(Philippians 2:3-4, ESV).

Grace

At a White House dinner, a lady was seated at the table and
noticed what she thought was a waiter standing behind her.
She requested a glass of wine, which he promptly obtained for her.

When he returned with her wine, she discovered he was not a
waiter. He was a four-star general!

He could have corrected her; he could even have been rude.
Instead, he graciously diffused her embarrassment, and everyone
had a good laugh.

What prompted this powerful man to act as a servant? Self-
sacrifice. Instead of taking offense, he empathized with her and
found a way to bring grace to the table.

Every day, we are presented with opportunities to take offense or
to bring grace. Maybe it's while you are on the road, fighting
traffic. Or maybe you are having trouble getting along with a
coworker or a friend.

Extend grace today.

There are no limits to caring ®

March 26

But Moses' hands grew weary, so they took a stone and put it under him, and he sat on it, while Aaron and Hur held up his hands... (Exodus 17:12, ESV).

Asking for Help

Joe was on a business trip, driving through Texas when he became distracted from the road and collided with a truck carrying a horse.

Several weeks later he tried to collect damages for his injuries. But the insurance company's lawyer was disputing his claim. "How can you now claim to have all these injuries? According to the police report, at the time of the accident you said you were not hurt."

Joe explained, "I was laying on the road in a lot of pain, and I heard someone say that the horse had a broken leg. The next thing I know this Texas Ranger pulled out his gun and shot the horse. Then he turned to me and asked, 'Are you okay?'"

Sometimes it seems safer to keep our pain to ourselves. But there is someone who cares about your pain. Find that caring friend. Or be that safe friend.

There are no limits to caring ®

March 27

Cast your bread upon the waters, for you will find it after many days (Ecclesiastes 11:1, ESV).

Josh

Our son Josh and his friend Tenley were both about 6 or 7 years old when they decided to go into business for themselves. It was in the fall of the year, when the decision was made to sell leaves to the neighbors for 25 cents each. So, off they went with a basket of leaves.

You get the picture. The economics of supply and demand were working against them. At each house, the neighbors kindly replied, "No thanks, we have all the leaves we need." I admired these kids at a young age – being innovative - but sometimes even the best of economic planning does not work.

Neither kid was set back by this experience. They showed initiative, they learned a lesson, and they met a lot of nice people along the way. That is life – for them and for us.

There are no limits to caring ®

March 28

The grass withers, the flower fades, but the word of our God will
stand forever (Isaiah 40:8, ESV).

Daylily

Have you seen a daylily lately? These beautiful flowers are appropriately named daylily; they bloom at sunrise and wither at sunset. Such beauty…but only for a day! And then they are gone!

A butterfly is similar to a daylily. When this beautiful creature finally emerges from its cocoon as a beautiful butterfly, it only lives for a short time. Such beauty…but only for a few days! And then it's gone!

We too are like the daylily and butterfly. Our lifetime will pass quickly. But while we are here, we are to bloom where we are planted. Such beauty… but only for a short time! And then we're gone from this earth.

But until then, bloom with kindness, love, compassion, caring and giving. What beauty! Be beautiful today, where you are. And your world will be beautiful too. What a real fashion statement!

There are no limits to caring ®

March 29

So, if the Son sets you free, you will be free indeed
(John 8:36, ESV).

Freedom

Harry Houdini became famous by boasting he could break out of any jail in the country. Wherever he took his act, he would go to the local jail and ask to be locked in. He would take a very strong and flexible piece of metal from his belt and then proceed to pick the lock.

It worked every time but one. On that occasion he labored for hours, but he just couldn't get the lock to cooperate. Finally, bathed in sweat and totally exhausted, he slumped against the door…and it swung open! It never had been locked. But in the Great Houdini's mind, it WAS locked, and that's all it took to keep him from opening the door.

So many of the things that hold us captive are just like that. The locks and chains are often only in our minds. With the right push, we can be set free to experience life to the fullest.

There are no limits to caring ®

March 30

*Are not five sparrows sold for two pennies? Yet not one of them
is forgotten by God. Indeed, the very hairs of your head are all
numbered. Don't be afraid; you are worth more than many
sparrows* (Luke 12:6-7, NIV).

You Are Special

A popular speaker held up a $20 bill, and asked, "Who would like this $20 bill?" Hands went up everywhere.

He then crumpled the bill and asked, "Now, who still wants it?" All hands went up. He then dropped it, and ground it into the floor with his foot, so that the bill was not only crumpled, but also dirty. "Now who wants it?" All hands went up.

He then said, "You've learned a great lesson. No matter what I did to the money, you still wanted it, because you knew it was still worth $20.

Many times in our lives we are dropped, crumpled, and ground into the dirt by the decisions we make or others make for us or due to the circumstances of life. But no matter what happens, you will never lose your value in the eyes of God and those who love you. You have value, you are special. Never forget it.

There are no limits to caring ®

March 31

It is a sin to despise one's neighbor, but blessed is the one who is kind to the needy (Proverbs 14:21, NIV).

Language of Kindness

C.N. Bovee said, "Kindness is a language which the mute can speak, the deaf can understand."

A student recently returned from a year and a half trip around the world on a tiny budget. His friends were amazed that he could have done it with little money and no language skills.

Wherever he went, he found people willing and ready to extend a helping hand.

--A Japanese woman who led him many blocks out of her way to an address he could never have found alone.
--An Indian family who shared fresh fruit with him on a ship from Mombasa to Bombay.
--An old Thai woman who brought him ice and delicious soups as he sweated through a three-day fever in her hotel.

Hundreds of people helped him when they sensed his need. He said, "The lack of verbal communication was no obstacle. It seems that kindness, like God's love, is a universal language."

There are no limits to caring ®

April 1

All who are prudent act with knowledge, but fools expose their folly (Proverbs 13:16, NIV).

Action

The photographer for a large magazine was assigned to get photos of a forest fire. But smoke at the scene hindered him from taking a good picture, so he asked his home office to hire a plane.

Arrangements were made and he was told to go immediately to the airport, where a plane would be waiting. When he arrived at the airport, he saw the plane warming up on the runway.

He jumped in and yelled, "Let's go! Let's go!" The pilot geared up, and they soon were in the air. "Fly over the north side of the fire," yelled the photographer, "and make three or four low passes."

"Why?" asked the pilot. "Because I'm going to take pictures," cried the photographer. The pilot gave him a strange look and said, "You mean you're not the flight instructor?"

Action without caution can be deadly. Think before you leap and don't fly by the seat of your pants.

There are no limits to caring ®

April 2

*God has been kind enough to trust us with this work. This is why
we never give up* (2 Corinthians 4:1, CEV).

Optimism

A father arrived at his son's little league game shortly after it begun. He approached his son sitting on the bench behind the first base line and asked what the score was. "We're behind, 12-0," he answered, grinning from ear to ear. "Really!" the father replied. "You don't look very discouraged." "Discouraged?" the boy asked with a puzzled look on his face. "Why should we be discouraged? We haven't even been up to bat yet."

Credit that youngster with optimism and certainly a winning spirit. The kind of attitude that makes all the difference.

Each new day is your opportunity to step up to bat. You may have strikes against you, you may have failures in your past.

But today is your opportunity to swing for the bleachers. Today, take your best swing, you could hit a home run. You won't know until you try.

There are no limits to caring ®

April 3

Children are a heritage from the LORD, offspring a reward from him (Psalms 127:2, NIV).

Worth Your Time

A man came home from work late, tired and irritated, to find his 5-year-old son waiting for him. "Daddy, how much do you make an hour?" the son asked.

"I make $50 dollars an hour," the father grumbled. "Well, can I borrow $25 dollars?" asked the son. The father angrily began to lecture his son on the value of money. He then ordered him straight to bed.

Later that evening, he began to wonder why his son wanted the money so badly. So, he went into his son's room and agreed to give him the money.

The little boy sat straight up, smiling. "Thank you, Daddy!" he yelled. Then, reaching under his pillow, he pulled out some money.

"Now I have $50 dollars. Can I please buy an hour of your time?"

How much is an hour with your son worth? Or your daughter, or wife? Prioritize your time, do what matters most.

There are no limits to caring ®

April 4

The LORD himself goes before you and will be with you; he will never leave you nor forsake you. Do not be afraid; do not be discouraged
(Deuteronomy 31:8, NIV).

John Deere

John grew up in Vermont in the early 1800's. The economy was struggling. Farmlands were destroyed by insects, and banks were collapsing.

When John was a child, his father died. His mother, living in poverty, raised him and his five siblings. In an effort to meet the needs of his family, John left home and took a job with a blacksmith.

Years later, he built his own blacksmith shop. But it burned down...twice...leaving him deeply in debt.

So, John moved to Illinois where he opened a blacksmith shop. He saw a need for plows and set to work to produce them. He sold only a few at first. But he kept improving his design, and years later, his shop became known as the John Deere Company.

When you work to meet the needs of others, even in difficult times, you will see great things happen. Keep the faith. Don't be discouraged

There are no limits to caring ®

April 5

Whoever is slow to anger has great understanding, but he who has a hasty temper exalts folly (Proverbs 14:29, NIV).

Temper

A young girl who had a bad temper was given a bag of nails by her mother. The mother told her daughter that every time she lost her temper, she must hammer a nail into the back of the fence. The first day, the girl had driven 37 nails into the fence.

As she learned to control her anger, the number of nails hammered declined. The day came when the girl didn't lose her temper at all. The mother suggested that her daughter pull out one nail for each day that she was able to hold her temper.

When all the nails were gone from the fence, the mother took her daughter by the hand and led her to the fence. She said, "You have done well, my daughter, but look at the holes in the fence. That fence will never be the same."

Anger is destructive. Learn to deal with your anger.

There are no limits to caring ®

April 6

Wait for the Lord; be strong and take heart and wait for the Lord
(Psalms 27:14, NIV).

Hang On

A bear was crossing a bridge, just minding his own business, when an oncoming car scared him. He jumped over the railing of the bridge, almost falling to his death.

He dangled for a while, clinging to a ledge beneath the bridge. After a few moments, he was able to claw his way back onto a concrete ledge.

At first, officials were not going to attempt a rescue. But the next morning, they found the bear still on the ledge, asleep. So, they decided to act.

They strung a net beneath the bridge and shot the bear with a tranquilizer dart. Once the bear fell unconscious, they pushed him into the net and later took him back to the forest to let him go.

Sometimes we are like that bear, just walking along, minding our own business, when life surprises us. But hang in there. Don't give up. Help will come…maybe a friend or family member…to catch us when we fall.

There are no limits to caring ®

April 7

Look to the LORD and his strength; seek his face always
(1 Chronicles 16:11, NIV).

Strength

In the past, many ships were lost in accidents at sea because they were overloaded. Too much stuff on the ship. The overloaded ships would disembark and as soon as the waters became rough, they would sink.

After several years of tragic losses, an Englishman named Plimsoll suggested that a line be painted on the sides of all ships so that it would be easy to tell when they were overloaded.

Soon, it became illegal for any ships to be loaded too heavily than allowed by the "Plimsoll mark." Do you know where your Plimsoll mark is?

What do you do when your load is too heavy? Turn to your faith, your friends, or just sink? When the storms come, we really can't manage an overloaded life.

Four guidelines for loading your ship:

- Don't carry more than you can
- Carry only what's important
- Know your limitations
- Learn to say "no, my ship is already loaded"

How heavy is your load today?

There are no limits to caring ®

April 8

Train up a child in the way he should go; even when he is old he will not depart from it (Proverbs 22:6, ESV).

Raising Up A Child

Growing Chinese bamboo requires patience, perseverance, and a large investment of time and labor. For the first year after planting, it is watered and fertilized every day. At the end of that year, the plant has grown to six inches. For the next five years, the plant is watered and fertilized daily. At the end of the fifth year, the plant is still only six inches tall! However, in the next five weeks, it will grow to the tremendous height of 90 feet!

During those first five years, the plant was developing a root structure. That sounds like good advice for raising children.

- Spend time with your child.
- Tell the child every day, often, I love you.
- Raise the child up in the teachings that God has taught us.

Then you know the child has an opportunity to be grounded and can grow to full potentials.

There are no limits to caring ®

April 9

Do not neglect to show hospitality to strangers, for thereby some have entertained angels unawares (Hebrews 13:2, ESV).

Kindness Lasts

An elderly gentleman told how he came to Portland, Oregon as a young man. Raised on a ranch in Montana, one of seven children, times were hard. In response to the conditions in Montana, he answered a "help-wanted" ad in a Portland paper. However, upon arriving in Portland, the store had gone out of business.

Since there were no other jobs in Portland, he started hitchhiking back to Montana, discouraged and broke. About a mile out of town, an elderly couple stopped and offered him a ride. Hearing his story, they suggested he stay with them and let them introduce him to their friends in the hope he would find a job.

Six weeks later, he was hired by one of the people he met. He concluded by saying, "I have lived happily in Portland for 78 years, and not a day goes by without remembering what that wonderful couple did for me."

The kindness that you give today will last a lifetime. Your kindness remembered will be an inspiration for others to be kind. One of the greatest motivations in our lives is the kindness that we receive from others. We are no doubt our best because of the kindness we have received from others as well as from Jesus. *"Be you kind, one to another."* (Ephesians 4:32)

There are no limits to caring ®

April 10

But as for you, be strong and do not give up, for your work will be rewarded
(2 Chronicles 15:7, NIV).

Thirsty Crow

A crow was in desperate need of water to drink. After searching for some time, he saw a pitcher of water sitting near a well.

Landing next to the pitcher, he eagerly put his beak into the mouth of the pitcher to drink. But when he did, he found that he could not reach far enough to drink the water.

He tried, and tried, but at last gave up. Almost at the point of despair, the crow sat down to rest. Then he had an idea. He took a pebble and dropped it into the pitcher.

Then he took another pebble and dropped it into the pitcher. He kept dropping pebbles into the pitcher until the water rose to the top of the pitcher. Then, he was at last able to drink and quench his thirst.

It's easy to give up when we don't see any progress. Find a creative way to make it happen. Don't quit!

April 11

If I have the gift of prophecy and can fathom all mysteries, and I have faith that can move mountains, but I do not have love, I am nothing
(1 Corinthians 13:2, NIV).

Kindness Remembered

A church organist tells of playing for two funeral services in one day. The one in the morning was for a very rich and powerful man. The one in the afternoon was for a sweet little old woman who lived in a poor section of town.

The morning funeral for the rich man was sparsely attended. People arrived silently and departed silently. The afternoon funeral had standing room only. After it was over, people stood in groups telling stories about how this poor woman had impacted their lives with many acts of kindness.

William Sloan Coffin said, "We are as we love. It is love that measures our stature."

A legacy of kindness and care expressed toward others will, in time and eternity, be seen as perhaps the greatest legacy of all. It costs nothing to share a cheerful greeting, extend our hand, and offer a word of encouragement. But it counts for so much.

There are no limits to caring ®

April 12

Tell it to your children, and let your children tell it to their children, and their children to the next generation (Joel 1:3, NIV).

The Price of Children

What is the latest calculation of the cost of raising a child from birth to 18? It is $245,000 for a middle-class family.

One e-mail raised the question, what do you get for your money?
-   Glimpses of God every day
-   More love than your heart can hold
-   A hand to hold...usually covered with jelly or chocolate
-   Someone to laugh yourself silly with, no matter what the boss said or how your stocks performed that day

You never have to grow up. You get to finger-paint, carve pumpkins, and play hide-and-seek.

You get to be a hero for retrieving a Frisbee off the roof, healing a boo-boo, and scaring away the monsters under the bed.

You get to be immortal. You get another branch added to your family tree, and if you're lucky, a long list of grandchildren and great grandchildren in your obituary.

That is quite a bargain! Love and enjoy your children, because they are a blessing.

There are no limits to caring ®

April 13

The years of our life are seventy, or even by reason of strength eighty . . . they are soon gone, and we fly away (Psalm 90:10, ESV).

Marbles

An elderly man gained a fresh perspective on priorities. Considering that the average person lives about seventy-five years, he multiplied 75 times 52 and came up with 3900. That's the number of Saturdays the average person can expect to have in a lifetime.

He was fifty-five years old before he thought about all of this. That meant he had already used up twenty-eight hundred Saturdays and had one thousand left. So, he bought one thousand marbles and put them in a clear plastic container. Each Saturday, he would throw away one marble. Watching those marbles diminish helped him focus on the really important things in life.

How are you going to spend this Saturday? Taking your wife out to breakfast? Spending time with your children? Maybe buy some marbles of your own? Whatever you do with this Saturday, make it count. More importantly, what will you do today?

There are no limits to caring ®

April 14

Serve wholeheartedly, as if you were serving the Lord, not people, because you know that the Lord will reward each one for whatever good they do (Ephesians 6:7-8, NIV).

The Boulder

In ancient times, a King placed a boulder on a roadway. He hid and watched to see if anyone would remove the huge rock. Some of his wealthiest merchants came by and simply walked around it. Many even blamed the king for not keeping the roads clear, but none tried to move it.

Then a peasant came along, carrying a load of vegetables. Upon approaching the boulder, he laid down his burden and tried to move the stone to the side of the road. After much pushing, he succeeded. He then picked up his load of vegetables and noticed a purse lying in the road where the boulder had been. The purse contained many gold coins and a note from the King indicating that the gold was for whoever removed the boulder from the roadway.

The peasant learned what many of us never understand. Every obstacle presents an opportunity to improve our condition.

April 15

*Farmers who wait for perfect weather never plant. If they watch
every cloud, they never harvest* (Ecclesiastes 11:4, NLT).

Procrastination

I have a friend who is a great procrastinator. He always puts
things off. He's good at it. He admits to being the biggest
procrastinator. He told me procrastinators are under rated because
procrastination is hard work. He said he had to put some tasks off-
-many times--before they slipped his mind--completely!

I also heard from another friend who moved near her sister. She
called countless times and asked the sister to meet her for lunch.
The sister always had an excuse.
- It wasn't a good time
- She had just washed her hair
- Or it looked like it might rain
- Or any one of a dozen excuses

She sadly related that her sister had died a few days ago. They
never did do lunch together.

Don't procrastinate. Take advantage of today's opportunities to
express your love and compassion, Today's opportunities are all
that we have...and remember, there are no limits to caring. Don't
procrastinate.

There are no limits to caring ®

118

April 16

Give us each day our daily bread (Luke 11:3, ESV).

One Day at a Time

Jesus taught his disciples to pray, *"Give us this day our daily bread."* And so it is with us. We have no assurance of tomorrow. And we certainly don't know what tomorrow will be like.

But our real opportunities are right here, right now. We can only live one day at a time. When we learn to live one day at a time, we stop taking our days for granted and experience life at a more meaningful level.

We have recently learned that we don't know what tomorrow will bring. This should bring a fresh appreciation for each moment we have. God has given us this day. It is a gift to be appreciated and enjoyed and used in a way that blesses.

"Give us this day our daily bread." May we eat it with joy and thanksgiving. May we understand that for this day, for this moment, there are no limits to caring.

There are no limits to caring ®

April 17

*In everything I did, I showed you that by this kind of hard work
we must help the weak, remembering the words the Lord Jesus
himself said: 'It is more blessed to give than to receive"* (Acts
20:35, NIV).

Greatest Moments

Marian Anderson was a great singer. A reporter once
interviewed her and asked her to name the greatest moment
in her life.

She had many great moments to choose from. There was that time
when she gave a private concert at the White House for the
Roosevelts and the King and Queen of England.

Or, there was that Easter Sunday in Washington D.C. when she
stood beneath the Lincoln statue and sang for a crowd of 75,000
people. Cabinet members, Supreme Court Justices, and most
members of Congress watched her perform that day.

Which of those big moments in her life did she choose? None.

Marian Anderson told the reporter that the greatest moment of her
life was the day that she went home and told her mother that she
wouldn't have to take in washing anymore.

The greatest things in life are not what we do for ourselves but what
we do for others.

There are no limits to caring ®

April 18

No one pours new wine into old wineskins. The wine would swell and burst the old skins. Then the wine would be lost, and the skins would be ruined. New wine must be put into new wineskins
(Mark 2:22, CEV).

Hunting Trip

Two men chartered a small plane to take them to the mountains of Canada to hunt moose. They managed to bag six moose. As they began to load the plane, the pilot stopped them, saying the plane could only hold four moose. The two men objected saying, "But last year, the pilot let us take all six, and he had the exact same plane as yours."

Reluctantly, the pilot gave in, allowed the men to load all six moose and the plane took off. While flying over the mountain range, the little plane couldn't handle the load and went down.

Surrounded by the moose bodies, the men and pilot managed to survive the crash. Climbing out of the wreckage, Pat said, "Any idea where we are?" Mick replied, "I think we're close to where we crashed last year."

Nothing changes until something changes.

There are no limits to caring ®

April 19

Greet one another with the kiss of love. Peace to all of you who are in Christ (1 Peter 5:14, ESV).

Embrace

I read an article with a picture showing infant twins lying face down in an incubator. One had its arm around the other. The article was entitled, *The Rescuing Hug*. The article details the first week of life of the set of twins.

Apparently, each were in different incubators, and one was not expected to live. A hospital nurse fought against the rules and placed the babies together in one incubator. When they were placed together, the healthier one threw an arm over her sister, embracing her. The smaller baby's heart rate stabilized, and her temperature rose to normal.

This is really not surprising. Human beings are designed to respond favorably to an appropriate touch. Study after study has been conducted showing that people who get regular hugs are healthier than those who are isolated from other human contact.

Don't forget to hug someone you love today.

There are no limits to caring ®

April 20

Now faith is the assurance of things hoped for, the conviction of things not seen (Hebrews 11:1, NIV).

Expect the Best

Since the teacher had no feedback from the principal, she felt she had done a poor job and would not be offered a second-year contract.

When she turned in her books to the principal, he told her he was looking forward to her return. He said, "Your students made the highest scores on the achievement test of any class in 10 years." She said, "Oh that was easy when you have students with IQ scores of 141, 152, 160, 155." The principle interrupted, "Those were not IQ scores given to you at the beginning of the year. Those were the numbers on their lockers."

The teacher had believed and expected the best from the students. She worked hard – believing she was teaching a class of geniuses. But believing in the students was more important than their IQ. Find a way to believe in one another.

There are no limits to caring ®

April 21

Do not be anxious about anything, but in every situation, by prayer and petition, with thanksgiving, present your requests to God. And the peace of God, which transcends all understanding, will guard your hearts and your minds in Christ Jesus (Philippians 4:6-7, NIV).

Owl Attacks

During the winter, the snow in Maine is thick on the ground. Cross-country skiing at night is a popular sport. On peaceful, moonlit nights, avid skiers would ski through the beautiful countryside. But lately, they were being targeted by a very cranky owl.

Skiers have reported that a great horned owl swooped down from the trees with talons outstretched and smacked them on the head.

There was no sound when the owl flew. Because of this, the skiers never even heard the owl coming. They were just happily skiing when, seemingly out of nowhere, the owl attacked.

Seems the owl was very territorial, and once skiers had moved through his territory, the owl left them alone.

In life, sometimes out of nowhere, difficulties catch you by surprise. Like the skiers, you didn't see it coming. Keep moving; look for solutions; and you find a path as you move through uncertain times.

There are no limits to caring ®

April 22

Then Peter came to Jesus and asked, "Lord, how many times shall I forgive my brother or sister who sins against me? Up to seven times?" Jesus answered, "I tell you, not seven times, but seventy-seven times (Matthew 18:21-22, NIV).

Sand and Stone

Two friends, Jim and Bob, were traveling through the desert. They had been lost several days and were irritable. They soon got into an argument, and Jim slapped Bob. Bob was hurt. So, he stooped down and wrote in the sand, "Today, my best friend slapped me."

Later, they came to an oasis where Bob, the one who was slapped, got in the water and almost drowned. His friend Jim did not hesitate to pull him out. After he recovered, Bob carved on a stone, "Today, my best friend saved my life."

Jim asked, "Why did you write on sand before and now on stone?" Bob replied, "When someone hurts us, we should write it down in sand where the winds of forgiveness can erase it away. But when someone does something good for us, we must engrave it in stone where no wind can ever erase it."

That's good advice. Learn to write your hurts in sand and carve your blessings in stone.

There are no limits to caring ®

April 23

Do you not know that in a race all the runners run, but only one gets the prize? Run in such a way as to get the prize. (1 Corinthians 9:24, NIV)

Mikey's Goal

The coach for a little league soccer team was very proud of his team. It was the final quarter of the last game of the season and the score was 2-1, his team leading.

With seconds remaining, the ball rolled in front of one of his players, Mikey. With shouts of "Kick it!" echoing across the field, Mikey reared back and gave it everything he had. All around, the crowd erupted. Mikey had scored!

Then there was silence. Mikey had scored in the wrong goal. Mikey has Down's syndrome and, for him, there is no such thing as a wrong goal.

The silence was finally broken when Mikey hugged one of his teammates and yelled, "I scored! Everybody won!" The teammate threw up his hand in the high-five salute and started chanting, "Way to go Mikey!" Within moments, both teams surrounded Mikey, joining in the chant and congratulating him on his goal.

The coach had never been prouder and neither had Mikey! Mikey may have scored the wrong goal but he made everybody on the field that day a winner. Go and do likewise! Everyone wins!

There are no limits to caring ®

April 24

You will be enriched in every way to be generous in every way,
which through us will produce thanksgiving
(2 Corinthians 9:11, ESV).

Emptiness in Your Life

A teacher was giving a lesson on the circulation of the blood. Trying to make the matter clearer, he said, "Now, boys, if I stood on my head, the blood, as you know, would run into it, and I would turn red in the face. When I am upright in the ordinary position, why doesn't the blood run into my feet?" A little boy shouted, "Cause your feet ain't empty."

What's empty in your life? Certainly not your head or feet! But what about your heart? Is there an emptiness there, a search for meaning and purpose? Why not look to those about you – those in need of a friend or food or clothing or just a genuine relationship. As you give to others, your heart takes on new meaning. And it is only in giving that we begin to receive – and the emptiness evaporates.

April 25

If you have raced with men on foot and they have worn you out,
how can you compete with horses? If you stumble in safe country,
how will you manage in the thickets by the Jordan? (Jeremiah
12:5, NIV).

In Personal Storms

It is not in the calm waters that the sailor learns to master the sea. It is during the storms that he learns to master his skills. And so it is with our lives. We may never know our strength until we face the test. The real test for a new ship is in the water, the real test for a new airplane is in the air, the real test for a new quarterback is on the football field, and the real test for you and me is often found in those difficult circumstances of life.

Difficult tests help build our confidence that we can handle tomorrow. As we work through difficulties, we gain mental and spiritual strength. Smooth sailing may be pleasurable, but it doesn't build character or courage. Facing and working through the storms of life not only strengthens our faith, but also offers encouragement to others as well.

April 26

A happy heart makes the face cheerful, but heartache crushes the spirit (Proverbs 15:13, NIV).

Expression

Many people say, "Of all the things you wear, your expression is the most important." That statement is really true.

Consider for a moment the value of a smile. When someone smiles at you, doesn't it usually cause you to receive them well? And doesn't a frown on another person's face bring you down just a bit? Just think, today, your smile could be the brightest part of someone's life.

You might not be able to afford the latest in designer wear or make a glamorous fashion statement. But how much does it cost to smile? That's really the best of all fashion statements. That's when you look your best.

Smiling is beneficial to others but also to ourselves. Research has shown that when you smile often, your brain rewires itself to create positive patterns more than negative ones. This creates a happier life. So remember.....Smile!

There are no limits to caring ®

April 27

*Know this, my dear brothers and sisters: everyone should be
quick to listen, slow to speak, and slow to grow angry*
(James 1:19, CEB).

Roosevelt

There is a story told of Franklin Roosevelt, who often had to endure long receiving lines at the White House after receptions or ceremonies.

His complaint was that in those receiving lines, no one really paid any attention to what was said. So, one day during a reception, he decided to try a bold experiment.

To each person who passed down the line and shook his hand, he mumbled with a smile, "I killed my grandmother this morning." The guests responded with smiles and phrases like, "Wonderful! Keep up the good work. We are proud of you. God bless you, sir."

It was not until the end of the line that he was actually heard. As he greeted the ambassador from Bolivia with the same statement, the ambassador leaned over and whispered to Roosevelt, "I'm sure she had it coming."

Do you really hear what is said? Listen closely; you may be surprised by what you hear. There are no limits to caring.

There are no limits to caring ®

April 28

People who conceal their sins will not prosper, but if they confess and turn from them, they will receive mercy (Proverbs 28:13, NLT).

Mistakes

Susan prepared homemade pasta for a dinner party she was giving. She had gone to great lengths to ensure that everything was just right. However, in her haste, she forgot to refrigerate the sauce, and it sat on the counter all day.

She was worried about spoilage, but it was too late to cook another batch. So, she called the local Poison Control Center and voiced her concern about the pasta sauce.

They suggested that Susan make a new batch. But she did not have time so she boiled the sauce, hoping it would kill any bacteria. That evening, the phone rang during dinner, and a guest answered it.

Her face dropped as she called out, "It's the Poison Control Center. They want to know how the spaghetti sauce turned out."

We all make mistakes. It's what we do with them that makes the difference. Deal with them or pretend they never happened. To pretend will be poisonous to everyone.

April 29

Jesus looked at them and said, "With man this is impossible, but with God all things are possible" (Matthew 19:26, ESV).

Spectacular Coincidence

Harry Parr Davies, a musical director, was on board the Queen Mary. One afternoon, he was leaning over the ship's rail and his eyeglasses fell off, dropping overboard.

He sent his assistant to the shop on board to buy another pair. There she saw a notice on the wall. It read, "Found...a pair of eyeglasses." The description sounded like the lost glasses, so she brought him to examine them.

Mr. Davies tried them on and discovered, to his amazement, that they were his own eyeglasses. Curious, he asked the shopkeeper about the man who had found them.

The man had been in his cabin on a lower deck. He had opened his porthole and put his hand out to see if it was raining. That's when a pair of glasses suddenly fell into his hand.

When life goes your way, and things seem to fall into place, enjoy every moment. Give thanks.

There are no limits to caring ®

April 30

He calmed the storm to a whisper and stilled the waves. What a blessing was that stillness as he brought them safely into harbor! (Psalms 107:29-30, NLT).

Changing the Storm

The sign read, "We can't direct the wind, but we can adjust the sails." That's especially true for today and every day.

There are many things in life that we have no power to change. There are some things we simply cannot change. We can't change the weather. We can't redirect a hurricane or change the force of the tide.

On the other hand, there are some things we can change. We can change our response to the storms of life. Our response will make all the difference!

We can refuse to panic; we can stay calm in the face of the unknown. We can respond to our neighbor in kindness.

We can be patient with one another. We can give a helping hand and be more concerned for others than ourselves. No, we can't control the storm, but we can control our response.

There are no limits to caring ®

May 1

In vain you rise early and stay up late, toiling for food to eat—for he grants sleep to those he loves (Psalm 127:2, NIV).

Sleeping Through Storms

A farmer owned land along the Atlantic coast. He constantly advertised for help. But people were reluctant to work on farms along the Atlantic because of the constant storms.

Finally, a man approached the farmer. "Are you a good worker?" the farmer asked. "Well, I can sleep when the wind blows," answered the man. His answer puzzled the farmer, but he was desperate for help, so he hired him and found he was a hard worker.

Then one night, a storm came ashore. The farmer rushed to the hired hand's room and woke him. The worker said, "I told you, I can sleep when the wind blows."

Enraged by the response, the farmer hurried outside to prepare for the storm. To his amazement, he discovered that the cows were in the barn, the doors were barred, and everything was tied down.

When you're prepared, spiritually, mentally, and physically, you have nothing to fear and can sleep when the wind blows through your life.

There are no limits to caring ®

May 2

Make the most of every opportunity in these evil days
(Ephesians 5:16, NLT).

Seize the Day

A young soldier and his commanding officer boarded a train. Sitting across from them was an attractive young woman and her grandmother. The soldier and the young woman kept eyeing each other – obviously attracted.

Suddenly, the train went into a tunnel. Immediately, two sounds were heard: the "smack" of a kiss and the "whack" of a slap.

The grandmother thought, "He kissed my granddaughter, but I'm glad she slapped him." The commanding officer thought, "I'm glad that soldier kissed that girl, but she missed his face and slapped me instead." The young girl thought, "I'm glad he kissed me, but I wish my grandmother hadn't slapped him for it."

When the train broke into the sunlight, the young soldier couldn't stop smiling. He had just seized the opportunity to kiss a pretty girl *and* slap his commanding officer!

Although the young soldier may have done wrong, he seized the opportunity. Today, seize the opportunity to do good!

There are no limits to caring ®

May 3

Love each other as brothers and sisters and honor others more than you do yourself (Romans 12:10, CEV).

Competition

We experience competition in a lot of places. On the athletic field, in the business world, the stock market, and even in churches and faith-based groups. Competition in the right place has made our country strong and a leader among all nations.

However, competition in the wrong place, such as the family, can be very harmful. Too often, we see kids competing for the parents' attention. Too often, we see husbands and wives competing with each other.

There is really no room for competition in the family. Instead of being competitors, family members need to be supporters. Competition usually means there will be a loser. In the family, we don't need a loser. When family members support each other, it becomes a win/win for everyone.

In the family, when we help each other become winners, we demonstrate there are no limits to caring.

There are no limits to caring ®

May 4

*So, I do not run aimlessly; I do not box as one beating the air. But
I discipline my body and keep it under control, lest after
preaching to others I myself should be disqualified*
(1 Corinthians 9:26-27, ESV).

Rose

At the age of 87, Rose went back to college. She said, "I have always dreamed of having a college education and now I'm getting one."

At a college football banquet that year, Rose said, "We do not stop playing because we are old; we grow old because we stop playing. There are only four secrets to staying young, being happy, and achieving success."

"You have to laugh and find humor every day. You've got to have a dream. When you lose your dreams, you die. Grow up by always finding the opportunity in change. Have no regrets. The elderly usually don't have regrets for what we did, but rather for things we did not do."

One week after graduation, Rose died peacefully in her sleep. She taught by example that it's never too late to be all you can possibly be!

There are no limits to caring ®

May 5

And we know that God causes everything to work together for the good of those who love God and are called according to his purpose for them (Romans 8:28, NLT).

Survivor

The only survivor of a shipwreck was washed up on an uninhabited island. After wandering the island, he found no shelter and had to build a small hut and gather food.

Every day, he prayed to be rescued, and every day he scanned the horizon for help...but it never came. Then one day, he left his fire burning in his hut and went out searching for food as was his routine. Upon returning home, he found his little hut in flames, the smoke billowing up to the sky.

He was angry and despondent. He'd lost all hope of rescue. But the next morning, he was awakened by the sound of a ship approaching the island. It had come to rescue him!

When he asked his rescuers how they had found him, they told him that they'd seen his smoke signal.

Prayers aren't always answered the way we expect. But even in our most hopeless moment, God is at work.

There are no limits to caring ®

May 6

Therefore, I urge you, brothers and sisters, in view of God's mercy, to offer your bodies as a living sacrifice, holy and pleasing to God—this is your true and proper worship
(Romans 12:1, NIV).

Blind

There was a girl who was blind and hated herself because she was blind. She hated everyone but her loving boyfriend, who was always there for her. She told him, "If only I could see, I would marry you."

One day, someone donated a pair of eyes for her. She was able to see everything, including her boyfriend. He asked her to marry him, now that she could see.

But when she looked at him, she saw he was blind. The sight of his closed eyelids shocked her. She hadn't expected that. The thought of looking at them the rest of her life led her to refuse to marry him. Her boyfriend left in tears.

Days later, he wrote her a note, "Take good care of your eyes, my dear, for before they were yours, they were mine."

Sacrifice …a mother, a father, or a friend…. Someone sacrificed much so you could be blessed! Don't take sacrifices for granted

There are no limits to caring ®

May 7

These commandments that I give you today are to be on your hearts. Impress them on your children. Talk about them when you sit at home and when you walk along the road, when you lie down and when you get up (Deuteronomy 6:6-7, NIV).

Protecting the Family

As I have watched birds this spring and summer, I have noticed on several occasions smaller birds, like mockingbirds, chase larger birds, like hawks. How could the smaller birds ever expect to win against such huge birds?

Do you know what the little birds were doing? Protecting their young, their family. That's what a parent is all about, protecting the family from those giant forces that would destroy the family.

In our culture, those giants include drug and alcohol abuse, pornography, selfishness, and materialism, to name a few.

You can be assured that every day, the big birds are out there trying to destroy your family. We must devote our time and energy to protecting the family. Those small birds provide a good model. When I saw them, the large birds were in retreat.

Because there are no limits to caring, we will continue to fight the giants. Make this a family day.

There are no limits to caring ®

May 8

... Love covers a multitude of sins (1 Peter 4:8, ESV).

Forever

A single mom was having major problems with her teen-age daughter. One night, the police called her to come pick up her daughter, who had been arrested for drunk driving.

The mother and daughter didn't speak until the next afternoon. Mom broke the tension by giving the daughter a gift. The daughter opened it and found a small rock inside. She rolled her eyes and said, "Cute Mom, what's this for?"

"Read the card," Mom said. Her daughter read the card and began to cry. She rushed to her mom and gave her a big hug. The card read, "This rock is 200 million years old. That's how long it'll take before I give up on you."

There is something powerful and compelling about a love that just won't quit. It's that kind of love that makes a difference. It offers hope and confidence.

Relationships can grow, when there are no limits to caring.

There are no limits to caring ®

May 9

*Honor your father and your mother, that your days may be long
in the land that the LORD your God is giving you*
(Exodus 20:12, ESV).

Andy Roddick

Several years ago, there was a hotel fire in Rome and three people were killed. Andy Roddick, the number two tennis player in the world at that time, was in that hotel.

He pulled twelve people into his room from the smoke-filled hallway. One person he caught in his arms as he leaped from the seventh floor to Roddick's sixth floor balcony. He summoned a fire truck ladder to move all thirteen people to safety.

During this entire ordeal, he used his one lifeline—he called his mama in Florida. She offered advice. He listened. She was amazed at his calmness.

As he moved all thirteen to safety, her heart swelled with pride when she heard him say, "I'll be the last one down."

She raised him right. He was never too big that he didn't need his mama.

Don't wait until your hotel catches on fire to call your mama. Do something special for her this Mother's Day.

There are no limits to caring ®

May 10

Children are a blessing and a gift from the LORD
(Psalms 127:3, CEV).

Helicopter Parents

We have all heard of soccer moms. Now there is a new one, helicopter parents. Like a helicopter, they hover over their children at a young age and even when they become adults.

Susan's mother attended job fairs with her daughter, handing out resumes, and even calling potential employers. She then challenged the employer when her daughter was not hired. These helicopter parents seek to prevent harm from coming to their children or letting them learn from their mistakes. Hodding Carter, Jr. said, "There are two lasting bequests we can give our children. One is roots, the other is wings."

Roots
- Values that give stability
- Honesty, integrity
- Staying the course through the storms

And Wings
- To leave the nest
- To create a life of their own
- To soar to new heights

That's our job as parents, to give roots and wings, not to hover. Some children never see their parents, while some can never escape the hovering of helicopter parenting.

There are no limits to caring ®

May 11

And it came to pass… (Exodus 12:41, ESV).

It Came to Pass

Several friends gathered one evening, discussing their thoughts about life. Each presented their favorite saying about life. But Ed, who was known for his simple wisdom, gave an intriguing message. "My favorite saying is from the Bible: *And it came to pass…*" His friends were amazed: why would this scholar pick such meaningless words? He could have picked a more famous verse like, "Love your neighbor as yourself."

But he explained, "*And it came to pass…* gives me hope."

"When life gets me down, this scripture reminds me
- That everything passes
- That life goes on, and so must I
- That we take the bad along with the good
- That this moment will pass and what I do with this moment makes all the difference
- That no matter how difficult the days, they too will pass."

Our challenge is to live in the moment—no matter the circumstances.

May 12

Do not be deceived: God cannot be mocked. A man reaps what he sows (Galatians 6:7, NIV)

Reap and Sow

Farmer Smith was a cranky fellow. And he didn't care for the little boy, Jacob, who lived next door. And Jacob, likewise, did not care for the ornery old farmer.

One day, young Jacob decided to take some grass seeds and scatter them over Farmer Smith's field, hoping that it would ruin his crops.

And it did. For years, the grass flourished. No matter how hard Farmer Smith tried, he couldn't get rid of the grass that eventually overtook his land.

Years later, Jacob grew into a young man and he noticed Farmer Smith's daughter was very lovely. So, he began talking to the farmer's daughter, and wouldn't you know it…they got married.

Many years later, Farmer Smith died, and Jacob and his wife inherited the farmer's property…as well as the large grassy field behind the house.

Remember, you reap what you sow.

There are no limits to caring ®

May 13

Learn to do right; seek justice. Defend the oppressed. Take up the cause of the fatherless; plead the case of the widow (Isaiah 1:17, NIV).

Tooth Fairy

Steven took lunches to elderly shut ins. He would often take his five-year-old daughter with him. She was always intrigued by the various tools of old age---the canes, walkers, and wheelchairs. One day, Steven noticed his daughter staring at a pair of false teeth soaking in a glass. As the father braced himself for what his daughter might say, she merely turned and whispered, "The tooth fairy will never believe this!"

Some things in life are unbelievable for a five-year-old or for a fifty-year-old.

You would never believe the number of people who every day reach out in kindness to others or the number of elderly people who just need someone to come by. You would never believe the number of children in this state who live in poverty.

You would never believe the difference you can make, until you reach out to another and see there are no limits to caring.

There are no limits to caring ®

May 14

Therefore, keep watch, because you do not know on what day your Lord will come (Matthew 24:42, NIV).

McKinley

One day before William McKinley became the 25th President of the United States, he interviewed two men for a job. Both men were equally qualified. He struggled to know which person to hire.

That evening, McKinley boarded a crowded streetcar on his way home from work. One of the men that he was considering was also aboard and did not see McKinley.

Just then, an old woman carrying a basket of laundry struggled into the car, searching for a seat. The job candidate pretended not to see her and kept his seat. McKinley gave up his seat to the old woman.

Right then, McKinley decided against hiring the man on the streetcar. He called it a "little omission of kindness."

Our decisions, even the small ones, tell a lot about us…even when we think no one is watching. A little omission of kindness may cost you more than you know.

May 15

*A body is made up of many parts, and each of them has its own
use. That's how it is with us. There are many of us, but we each
are part of the body of Christ, as well as part of one another*
(Romans 12:4-5, CEV).

Redwood Trees

Not long ago, we visited the huge redwood forests of
California. These huge trees are amazing. They are the
largest living things on earth and the tallest trees in the world.
Some of them have grown to 300 feet high and are over 2,500
years old.

One would think that trees this large must have a massive root
system that reaches down hundreds of feet into the soil. But in
fact, the redwoods have a very shallow root system.

Their root system is shallow…but all their roots intertwine with
each other. They are locked together with the other redwoods in
the forest. When the storms come, they still stand. All the trees
support and protect each other.

In the same way, we are like the giant redwood trees. We need
each other – our family, friends, and neighbors - to be a support
system. Then, when the strong winds of life blow, we can hold
each other up.

There are no limits to caring ®

May 16

As far as east is from west—that's how far God has removed our sin from us (Psalm 103:12, CEB).

Priest Retirement

A priest was being honored at his retirement dinner. A member of the congregation was to give a little speech at the dinner. The speaker was delayed, so the priest decided to say a few words while they waited.

The priest began by telling the congregation about the challenges he had faced on his first day at the parish. The very first person who came to confession, he said, had stolen a television set, embezzled money, had an affair, and taken illegal drugs.

Just as the priest finished his talk, the speaker arrived, apologizing for being late. He immediately began to make his speech.

"I'll never forget the first day our parish priest arrived," he began. "In fact, I had the honor of being the first one to go to him in confession."

Some things don't need to be revisited. Find forgiveness. Change your lifestyle. Move from the past and celebrate who God has created you to be.

There are no limits to caring ®

May 17

*For the sake of Christ, then, I am content with weaknesses,
insults, hardships, persecutions, and calamities. For when I am
weak, then I am strong*
(2 Corinthians 12;10, ESV).

Flaws

A man had two pots. Both hung on each end of a pole which he carried across his neck.
- One pot was perfect and always delivered a full portion of water at the end of the long walk from the stream to the house.
- However, the other pot was cracked, leaked along the way, and only arrived half full.

The perfect pot was proud of its accomplishments. But the poor cracked pot was ashamed of its flaw.

The man felt compassion for the cracked pot. He asked the pot to notice the flowers growing along beside the path. The man explained to the pot, "I planted seeds along the path. Each day, because of your flaw, the pot watered the seeds. And because of your flaw, we are able to enjoy these beautiful flowers."

Each of us has our own unique flaw. Acknowledge it and use it to create beauty all around you.

There are no limits to caring ®

May 18

You hypocrite, first take the plank out of your own eye, and then you will see clearly to remove the speck from your brother's eye.
(Matthew 7:5, NIV).

Hearing Problem

A man went to the doctor very concerned about his wife's hearing and her unwillingness to go to the doctor. He told the doctor the story. The doctor said, "I want you to go home tonight and do exactly what I'm about to tell you."

So, the man returned home and found his wife at the kitchen sink. From 20 feet away, he asked her, "Honey, what's for dinner?" No answer. He walked up 15 feet and asked the question. No answer. From 10 feet, no answer. Finally, the man got to 5 feet from his wife and asked again, "Honey, what's for dinner"? She turned around and responded, "For the fourth time…Lasagna!"

Sometimes, it's not the other person who has the problem… it's me. Be careful not to blame others for what we can't hear about ourselves. The Bible talks about seeing the flaws of others, yet not recognizing our own flaws.

There are no limits to caring ®

May 19

Yet you do not know what tomorrow will bring. What is your life? For you are a mist that appears for a little time and then vanishes (James 4:14, ESV).

Five More Minutes

A woman sat down next to a man near the playground. "That's my son," she said pointing to a child on the slide.

"That's my son on the swing," the man said. Then he called to his son and said, "Todd, it's time to go." "Just five more minutes," the little boy pleaded. The father agreed.

Later he called to his son again. Again, the boy asked for five more minutes, and the father agreed with a smile.

The woman commented, "You certainly are a patient father." The man replied, "My older son was killed in a car wreck last year. I never spent much time with him, and now I'd give anything for five minutes with him. I vowed not to do the same with Todd. He thinks he's getting five more minutes to play, but the truth is, I'm getting five more minutes to watch him."

Life is all about priorities. Evaluate your priorities today. Make time for the important people in your life.

There are no limits to caring ®

May 20

But seek first his kingdom and his righteousness, and all these things will be given to you as well (Matthew 6:33, NIV).

Priorities

One Sunday, a pastor at a rural church was invited for lunch at the home of a church member.

The mother was at the kitchen sink, washing dishes, when her little four-year-old boy came to her with a magazine. "Mommy," he asked, "what is this man in the picture doing?" To the pastor's surprise, the mother stopped what she was doing, dried her hands, and sat down on a chair. She then took her son in her lap and spent the next few minutes answering his questions.

After the child had left, the pastor commented on the mother's patience at being interrupted to answer the boy's question. "Most mothers wouldn't have done that," he said. "Well," replied the mother, "I expect to be washing dishes for the rest of my life, but never again will my son ask me that question."

Life is all about priorities. What are yours?

May 21

*For where jealousy and selfish ambition exist, there will be
disorder and every vile practice. But the wisdom from above is
first pure, then peaceable, gentle, open to reason, full of mercy
and good fruits, impartial and sincere*
(James 3:16-17, ESV).

Jealousy

Most children grow up with a fear of monsters. And we all know monsters aren't real. But there is one monster that is very much real...the green-eyed monster. Jealousy is typically a negative emotion with fear and anxiety.

And all of us encounter this monster. After all, this monster is all around us, waiting for an opportunity to pounce.

When someone experiences a success or even a blessing of some kind, we may be jealous. After all, it is easier to cry with someone than to celebrate with someone.

Like a small child, we may feel jealousy because of a sense of entitlement. Or maybe it's because we think we might lose something...like a spouse or a special toy. And the unfairness of life awakens the green-eyed monster from his deepest, darkest hiding place.

With trust and thanksgiving, we can pounce on the green-eyed monster defeating him in our lives.

There are no limits to caring ®

May 22

Gray hair is a crown of glory; it is gained in a righteous life
(Proverbs 16:31, ESV).

Not Disposable

We live in a "throw-away" culture. More and more things are made which are disposable…to be thrown away. Disposable diapers, disposable dinnerware, disposable paper and plastics… you name it! After they are used, they are thrown away.

Some things are not meant to be thrown away, no matter how old or worn they may become. Like friends… friends are not disposable. If you have good friends, you need to keep them. Or aging parents. You only get one set of parents. If you have them, treasure them and care for them. Neither is marriage something to throw away. A lengthy marriage represents years of investment and can accumulate great value.

Remember the value of the important things in life. Keep them. They often constitute God's greatest gifts. And be careful what you throw away. The best things in life often improve with age.

May 23

He lifted me out of the slimy pit, out of the mud and mire; he set my feet on a rock and gave me a firm place to stand (Psalm 40:2, NIV).

Lotus Flower

If you have seen a lotus flower, or a photograph of one, you know that it is a beautiful and colorful flower that blooms upon the surface of small bodies of water, particularly muddy waters.

Each morning it rises to the surface to bloom with breathtaking beauty. At night, the flower closes, sinking underwater, where it waits for dawn so it can rise to the surface again.

An ancient Chinese scholar said this about the lotus flower: "I love the lotus because while growing from mud, it is unstained." Throughout history, this flower has come to represent purity, beauty, and honor.

Every day, there are people in this community who have to overcome adverse surroundings. People living in poverty, children with incarcerated parents, children suffering abuse and neglect.

Each day, they must choose to rise above their circumstances in order to bloom.

There are no limits to caring ®

156

May 24

An excellent spirit, knowledge, and understanding to interpret dreams, explain riddles, and solve problems were found in this Daniel (Daniel 5:12, ESV).

Band-Aids

Earl Dickson was an employee of Johnson & Johnson. At that time, Johnson & Johnson only sold large surgical dressings in individual packages. But these were not very practical for small cuts and burns.

When a smaller bandage was needed, Earl Dickson placed a small wad of sterile cotton and gauze in the center of an adhesive strip to hold it in place. But Earl grew tired of making up these little bandages every time one was needed.

The company's president, James Johnson, noticed Dickson placing one of his homemade bandages on his finger. Impressed, he decided to start mass-producing them, and called them Band-Aids.

Dickson had been looking for a way to solve a small problem, and in the process, he invented a new product.

You too can solve problems. Find solutions. Don't give up when you see a need. Find a real solution, not just a Band-Aid.

There are no limits to caring ®

May 25

We who are strong have an obligation to bear with the failings of the weak, and not to please ourselves (Romans 15:1, ESV).

The Two Mules

A farmer was going to town one morning to sell his harvest. He had two carts loaded full of goods to sell at market. A mule was pulling each cart.

The first mule carried his cart with ease, but when he began to climb the steep path of the mountain, his load became more than he could bear.

He asked the second mule to relieve him of a small portion, so that he could carry the rest. But the second mule ignored the request, not wanting to be bothered.

The first mule, unable to bear his load any longer, fell down, dead, under the weight of his load. So, the farmer placed upon the second cart the entire load that had been on the first cart. And the second mule had to carry both loads by himself.

Every day, we pass people whose burdens are more than they can bear. Lend a helping hand to someone who has a load.

There are no limits to caring ®

158

May 26

For by you I can run against a troop, and by my God I can leap
over a wall
(Psalm 18:29, ESV).

Violin

Many years ago, Perlman, a violinist, performed at a concert in New York. About halfway through his performance, one of the strings on his violin broke.

The sound was heard throughout the auditorium, and the music came to a sudden stop.

The crowd waited for the string to be replaced, but one could not be found. To everyone's surprise, Perlman looked at his violin for a moment, studying it, and then nodded to the conductor to begin where the music had stopped.

For the rest of the concert, Perlman played on only three strings what should have been played on four.

The audience gave him a standing ovation for this amazing display of talent. Perlman humbly bowed and told the crowd, "Sometimes it is the job of the artist to find out how much music you can still make with what you have left."

Sometimes life brings the unexpected. But it's up to each of us to make beautiful music in difficult times.

There are no limits to caring ®

May 27

A friend nearby is better than relatives far away (Proverbs 27:10, CEV).

Man's Best Friend

Debbie Parkhurst was eating an apple at her home one afternoon when a piece got caught in her throat. As she began to choke, she tried to give herself the Heimlich maneuver, but it didn't work. After she began beating on her chest, her dog Toby noticed and got involved.

When Toby, a 2-year-old golden retriever, saw his owner choking on the fruit, he got up on his hind feet and put his front paws on her shoulders, pushing her to the ground. Stunned, Debbie was on her back as Toby began jumping up and down on her chest.

That's when the apple dislodged. Debbie believes her dog was trying to save her life.

She later said, "I literally have paw-print-shaped bruises on my chest. But I'm okay,"

No wonder they call them "man's best friend". A friend is someone who is there when you have need. With a loyal friend by our side, we can breathe a little easier.

There are no limits to caring ®

May 28

Better to be patient than powerful; better to have self-control than to conquer a city (Proverb 16:32, NLT).

Easy Now, Donald

A young father in a supermarket was pushing a shopping cart with his little son strapped in the front. The little boy was fussing, irritable, and crying. The other shoppers gave them stern looks because the child would pull cans off the shelf and throw them on the floor.

The father seemed very calm; as he continued down each aisle, he murmured gently: "Easy now, Donald. Keep calm, Donald. Steady boy. It's all right, Donald."

A mother who was passing by was greatly impressed by this young father's approach. She said, "You certainly know how to talk to an upset child—quietly and gently." And then bending down to the little boy, she said, "What seems to be the trouble, Donald?"

"Oh no," said the father. "He's David. I'm Donald."

We cannot control the way others behave, but only how we respond. These are definitely times we can say to ourselves, "easy now… keep calm…"

There are no limits to caring ®

May 29

*But the Lord said to Samuel, "Do not look on his appearance or
on the height of his stature, because I have rejected him. For the
Lord sees not as man sees: man looks on the outward
appearance, but the Lord looks on the heart"*
(1 Samuel 16:7, ESV).

Clay Vessels

A man was exploring caves by the seashore when he found
several hardened clay balls that had been rolled up and left to
bake in the sun.

They didn't look like much. So, he put them in a bag and, as he
walked along the beach, he would throw the clay balls into the
ocean.

Suddenly, he dropped one and it cracked open on a rock. Inside
was a beautiful, precious stone. The man broke open the remaining
clay balls and found treasures in each one.

But then it struck him. He had thrown many of the clay balls into
the ocean and had lost all those precious stones!

It's like that with people. We look at someone and see the external
clay vessel. We throw them away…write them off as if they have
no value.

But if we take the time to get to know that person, we will find a
beautiful treasure inside.

There are no limits to caring ®

May 30

Blessed is the man who remains steadfast under trial, for when he has stood the test he will receive the crown of life, which God has promised to those who love him
(James 1:12, ESV).

Stumbling Blocks

At times we are confronted with challenging moments in life: the death of a spouse, problems in the marriage, the struggles of parenting, financial crises, aging parents.

These difficulties are stumbling blocks for some or steppingstones for others. We choose which it will be by the way we walk. If we drag our feet in despondency, then the trials will certainly be stumbling blocks.

But if we pick our feet up and walk with thanksgiving and know by our faith that God will bring good out of evil, then what was a stumbling block becomes a steppingstone.

The circumstances that were to defeat us actually becomes defining moments that create new opportunities. How we respond determines the future. We can be bitter or better, we can stumble and fall, or we can use our trials as steppingstones. That's the choice that we will make today.

There are no limits to caring ®

May 31

[For everything there is a season] A time to cry and a time to laugh. A time to grieve and a time to dance (Ecclesiastes 3:4, NLT).

Taps

In 1862, Union Army Captain Robert Ellicombe, hearing the moans of a wounded man on the battlefield, crawled under cover of darkness to retrieve the confederate soldier. When he got him back to his own lines, the soldier was dead. To his horror, he discovered the young confederate was his son. The boy had been studying music in the South and had joined the Confederate army, without telling his father.

Ellicombe asked permission to give his son a full military funeral. Because his son was a Confederate, he was offered a single bugler. He asked him to play a series of notes he had found on a piece of paper in his son's pocket. The haunting melody, we now know as "*Taps.*"

We live in a world filled with wars. We hear those notes too often. We salute the brave men and women and their families for whom they play. And we offer our prayers.

There are no limits to caring ®

June 1

Then Peter came to him and asked, "Lord, how often should I forgive someone who sins against me? Seven times?" "No, not seven times," Jesus replied, "but seventy times seven!" (Mark 10:9, NIV).

Benefits of Forgiveness

When most people hear the word forgiveness, something inside of them cringes. We start thinking of all of the reasons this person does not deserve our forgiveness.

According to a study published in the Journal of Behavioral Medicine, forgiveness helps to reduce blood pressure and lower your heart rate. There are also psychological and spiritual benefits to releasing the negative emotions associated with un-forgiveness. An article on everydayhealth.com says that forgiveness is related to better sleep and supports a healthier immune system.

Be quick to forgive and also to ask for forgiveness.

Take it a step further to reach out with God's love to see what you can do to help that person on their road to healing. You just may be the person God wants to use to help that person to forgive and even find forgiveness.

There are no limits to caring ®

June 2

When they saw the courage of Peter and John and realized that
they were unschooled, ordinary men, they were astonished and
they took note that these men had been with Jesus
(Acts 4:13, NIV).

Qualified

Are you qualified for the job you are doing? Every employer wants qualified workers. Usually, that means someone who is trained and experienced. Many people fail to apply for certain jobs because they believe they are unqualified.

Think about this: When God asked Noah to build an Ark, he asked an amateur. Noah had never built one before and knew nothing about shipbuilding. No one did! There had never been an ark before! Noah did the best he could with what he had and launched a very successful shipbuilding operation! On the other hand, the Titanic was built by experienced professionals.

Remember that when you dream and aspire to attempt things you've not tried or done before. Too often people say, "I can't," and believe it – thus limiting their potential. Those two words, "I can't," should be used rarely when referring to what we are capable of doing. Remember Noah!

There are no limits to caring ®

June 3

He will yet fill your mouth with laughter and your lips with shouts of joy (Job 8:21, NIV).

A joyful heart is good medicine, but a crushed spirit dries up the bones (Proverbs 17:22, ESV).

Laughter

At our home we do a lot of laughing. Life is funny! The average adult laughs 17 times a day.

Sitcoms, jokes, and comedians are all designed to get us laughing, because laughing feels good.

Laughter says something is right in this relationship! The absence of laughter says something is not right. Laughter helps us relate to family—not to be so serious or heavy. It's a way to make us comfortable.

However, be careful that laughter is not a result of putting someone down. Laughter is a positive force. Keep it positive.

Laughter is healthy -- that's why we've all heard the saying, "Laughter is the best medicine." There is strong evidence that laughter can actually improve health and help fight disease.

Laughter is contagious. It releases stress, and laughter is good for the soul.Laugh right now…it's good for the soul.

There are no limits to caring ®

June 4

*You shall give to him freely, and your heart shall not be grudging
when you give to him, because for this the Lord your God will
bless you in all your work and in all that you undertake*
(Deuteronomy 15:10, ESV).

No Thanks

Doesn't it make you feel good to get a pat on the back, to have someone say "thank you" when you have done something worthwhile? It is great to be appreciated.

But what about when there is no gratitude? When you have helped someone, only to have him or her ignore it or act like it never happened. What is our response when there is no appreciation for the good we do? That can be downright painful.

It may be understandable when someone says, "I would help those folks, but they wouldn't appreciate it." But can we also understand that those are the very ones who need help the most? People who do not have the grace of gratitude desperately need to see the grace of giving.

Besides, it remains true: "It is more blessed to give, than to receive." It doesn't have to do with being thanked. It has to do with caring, and there are no limits to caring.

There are no limits to caring ®

June 5

*We give thanks to God always for all of you, constantly
mentioning you in our prayers* (1 Thessalonians 1:2, ESV).

Reason, Season, Lifetime

During our lifetime, we encounter many people. However, it is
unclear why certain people come into our lives and leave
without warning, while others remain for a lifetime.

It seems certain people are in our lives for a REASON. They meet
needs we have. They provide invaluable assistance. They aid us
physically, emotionally, or spiritually. They seem like a Godsend,
and they are.

Others come into our lives for a SEASON. They come and go, but
give opportunities to learn, grow, and share.

LIFETIME relationships teach us lifetime lessons. They allow us
to put to use all that we have learned about accepting others, loving,
and caring.

Look at the people in your life today, thank God for them, and
thank them for what they bring your way. Some are there for a
reason, some for just a season, some for a lifetime.

There are no limits to caring ®

June 6

We are hard pressed on every side, but not crushed; perplexed,
but not in despair; persecuted, but not abandoned; struck down,
but not destroyed
(2 Corinthians 4:8-9, NIV).

Carrot, Egg, Or Bean

It's been said that crises bring out the best in the best of us…and the worst in the worst of us.

If you place carrots in boiling water, they will get soft. Place eggs in boiling water, and they will get hard. Place coffee beans in boiling water, and you will get a rich and delicious drink of coffee.

Adversity comes to all of us. We don't have much choice about that. But we can ask ourselves if we want to be like a carrot, growing soft and weak when the times get tough. Or, do we want to be like an egg and when the heat is on, becoming hard-boiled. Or, do we want to be like coffee beans, letting the hot water produce something wonderful.

We often cannot choose our adversities. But we can choose how we respond.

There are no limits to caring ®

June 7

Do not neglect to do good and to share what you have, for such sacrifices are pleasing to God (Hebrews 13:16, ESV).

Giving or Blessing

My sister Martha taught 5-year-old kindergarteners in Lineville, Alabama. CNN News spent a day with her, covering her class, while her husband was involved in the Gulf War. During national coverage, children were coloring with crayons. Brad shared his color crayons with another child. Martha said to him, "Thank you, Brad, for sharing."

In New Jersey, Bill, watching this national broadcast on CNN, was touched by Brad's act of sharing. Bill began sending money to Martha for children who had special needs. That was a remarkable story, except it didn't end there. Bill continued to share money for two decades, until he died.

A five-year-old shared a color crayon and caused a man in New Jersey to share for the rest of his life. Unbelievable! Your kindness to will spread to others. Experience the joy of sharing. Just do it. Share.

There are no limits to caring ®

June 8

Good salt is worthless if it loses its saltiness; it can't season anything. So, don't lose your flavor! Live in peace with each other (Mark 9:50, TLB).

Salt

Salt is a wonderful commodity. It can be used as a preservative, when making pickles or curing meats. It can be used to melt ice and snow on highways. It can be used in making ice cream, causing the ice to melt and the water to get colder, which causes the ice cream to freeze more quickly. It is also used as a seasoning, making certain foods better.

Salt can do none of those things if left in its container. It has to be applied, to be poured out. Salt left in the saltshaker makes nothing better.

Like salt, each of us can work to preserve things of value. Each of us can influence, or "flavor," our surroundings for the better, but only if we get out of the shaker. Salt, just like all our good intentions, has to be applied in order to do any good.

Care enough to get out of the shaker.

There are no limits to caring ®

June 9

To those who by persistence in doing good seek glory, honor and immortality, he will give eternal life (Romans 2:7, NIV).

Green Beans

Do you have foods that you just don't really like, but make yourself eat them anyway? Former President George Bush, Sr. concluded he did not have to eat broccoli. After all, he was the president!

When I was in the first grade, we always got a star by our names on the day we ate all our lunch. That star was the only reason I ate green beans. Now, I love garden fresh green beans, but in the first grade, I ate them because I wanted a star!

Sometimes we do things we don't like to do – because it's the right thing to do. It's good for us. We may even get a star. But we really need to do the right thing even if no one is looking. There are many people in this community who demonstrate kindness – without ever getting a star, but what a difference they make.

There are no limits to caring ®

June 10

Let the wise hear and increase in learning, and the one who understands obtain guidance (Proverb 1:5, ESV).

I've Learned

What Andy Rooney wrote spoke to me:

I've learned…that the best classroom in the world is at the feet of an elderly person.

I've learned… that just one person saying to me, "You've made my day!" makes my day.

I've learned… that being kind is more important than being right.

I've learned… that I can always pray for someone when I don't have the strength to help him in some other way.

I've learned… that no matter how serious your life requires you to be, everyone needs a friend to act goofy with.

I've learned… that sometimes all a person needs is a hand to hold and a heart to understand.

I've learned… that life is like a roll of toilet paper. The closer it gets to the end, the faster it goes.

I've learned… that we should be glad God doesn't give us everything we ask for.

Most of these things I learned from my mama and daddy along the way. I just need to remember them!

There are no limits to caring ®

June 11

So, brothers, in whatever condition each was called, there let him remain with God (1 Corinthians 7:24, ESV).

Sweet Pea

Mary had just finished planting seeds for her new vegetable garden. She tended it carefully and waited for the seeds to sprout.

One morning, Mary spotted the tip of a sweet pea growing through the crack in the walkway. She figured it had probably been dropped by accident and wouldn't live very long, so she paid it no attention.

But to her surprise, the plant held on, struggling to grow taller every day. Each morning, it seemed to have grown and flourished. So, Mary placed a trellis near it in hopes that the vine would continue to grow.

And it did. Despite its hard beginning, it began to bud, and its blooms were more abundant and beautiful than any of the other plants in the garden.

You don't get to choose where you are planted, but if you refuse to give up, you will find the strength and courage to continue to grow, to bloom where you are planted.

There are no limits to caring ®

June 12

If then you have been raised with Christ, seek the things that are above, where Christ is, seated at the right hand of God. Set your minds on things that are above, not on things that are on earth (Colossians 3:1-2, ESV).

Ships

Two ships are at sea: one ship steers east, another west. The same breeze blows for both ships. It is the set of the sail and not the wind that determines the way the ships go.

We are like ships. It is the set of our sails that determines where we will go. Circumstances come and at times can be very difficult, if not devastating, but by and large what happens has everything to do with the way we handle the circumstances. As a result, we can either be bitter or better.

We need to deal with our circumstances in a positive way, so that our ship can sail where we want to go and not where the wind takes us. Where we set our sails determines our destiny.

June 13

A father to the fatherless, a defender of widows, is God in his holy dwelling (Psalm 68:5, NIV).

Father's Day

Some kids talked their mother into getting a hamster but only on the condition that the children took care of their new hamster...named Danny.

Danny was a lot of trouble and the kids soon forgot about him, so mom decided it was time to give Danny to a new owner.

When she told the children, one said, "I'll miss him, he's been around here a long time." Another child suggested he might be able to stay if he ate less and wasn't so messy.

But Mom was firm and said, "Let's go, it's time to take Danny to his new home." Then, in unison, the kids shouted, "Danny? We thought you said Daddy!"

Father's Day is a time to let your father know that you appreciate him and all he does. If you are without a father, remember Psalms 68:5 says, "a father to the fatherless, a defender of the widows, is God in His Holy Dwelling.

There are no limits to caring ®

June 14

Beware that you don't look down upon a single one of these little children. For I tell you that in heaven their angels have constant access to my Father (Matthew 18:10, TLB).

Scissors

When our daughter was five years old, we took her to kindergarten for an evaluation. She did really well except for one thing – scissors. She did not know how to use scissors.

Well, her dad had been a little overprotective, and wouldn't let her have scissors. I didn't want her punching her eye out, or cutting up her shirt, or my shirt. So, she had never used scissors before the age of five.

Sometimes in our struggle to protect our children, we can deny them the opportunity to grow and develop. And yet there are some things from which we need to protect them – drugs and pornography and violence... bullies. Finding the balance between healthy protection, and being overprotective, is a real challenge. However, struggling to find that balance shows that you really care about your kids. We need parents who demonstrate there are no limits to caring for our kids.

Have a great day protecting your kids.

There are no limits to caring ®

June 15

They encouraged the followers and begged them to remain faithful (Acts 14:22, CEV).

Belief

Who believes in you? We all need someone to believe in us no matter the circumstances.

When I was a child growing up, my dad always believed in me...even when it wasn't easy. Sometimes I had done the wrong thing or come close to being with the wrong crowd...yet he believed in me.

When I was a college student, a married couple (who later became my professors) believed that I could achieve more. They raised the bar for me...and believed in me. Even though one is deceased, his belief in me continues to be an encouragement to this day.

As an adult, my wife's constant belief in me motivates me to be my best. That makes all the difference in my life.

And because there have been people in my life who believe in me, I too can believe in others...regardless of the circumstances.

Believe in others and believe in yourself.

There are no limits to caring ®

June 16

Give, and it will be given to you. A good measure, pressed down, shaken together and running over, will be poured into your lap. For with the measure you use, it will be measured to you (Luke 6:38, NIV).

Good Deeds Returned

Victor and his wife were driving when they saw a car stopped along the side of the road.

So, Victor pulled over to help the driver, a woman named Lisa, change her tire. Lisa was grateful for Victor's help. When Victor finished, he went on his way.

But a few miles down the road, Victor began having chest pains. His wife guided the truck to the side of the road.

A moment later, another motorist saw Victor's truck stopped on the side of the road and pulled over to see if they needed help.

Could you believe it was Lisa? When she saw Victor having a heart attack, she began CPR until paramedics arrived.

Victor was flown to the hospital where he was treated. Doctors said if Lisa had not been there to administer CPR, Victor would not have survived.

A good deed always comes back to you.

There are no limits to caring ®

June 17

Two are better than one, because they have a good return for
their labor: If either of them falls down, one can help the other
up. But pity anyone who falls and has no one to help them up
(Ecclesiastes 4:9-10, NIV).

Pulling Together

A farmer had two horses that he used to pull plowing equipment. When the horses pulled separately, each only pulled about 4,000 pounds. But when the farmer put them together as a team, they pulled over 12,000 pounds! That is a 200% increase in capacity – just because they pulled together.

A family will always be stronger when the husband and wife are pulling together. A business will be stronger when the employees are pulling together. A community will be stronger when that community is pulling together.

The Bible says in Ecclesiastes 4:9-12 that "Two are better than one, because they have a good return for their labor."

Want to become part of a strong team? Want to make someone's life better every day? Visit our website or Facebook page to join our VOA team! Together, we can make a bigger difference!

There are no limits to caring ®

June 18

But they who wait upon the LORD shall renew their strength;
they shall mount up with wings like eagles; they shall run and not
be weary; they shall walk and not faint (Isaiah 40:31, ESV).

Holding Patterns

Last time I flew from Mobile to Atlanta, we ended up in a holding pattern just outside Atlanta. Sometimes in holding patterns, we experience turbulence when we are flying around a circle, and that's no fun.

You know, life has its own "holding patterns' as well.

- Like when you are waiting on the doctor's diagnosis
- Or you pray to be healed, and nothing happens
- When you are having problems with your children, or in your marriage, and you are waiting on a solution
- When you are looking for a job, knocking on doors, but nothing yet
- Or like when the world is up and down, causing us to ask, "What's next?"

Holding patterns. They're no fun.

However, holding patterns can be productive if we will use the time to think, meditate, and pray. Make sure you have done your best and trust the matter into the hands of others and into God's hands.

There are no limits to caring ®

June 19

Consider it pure joy, my brothers and sisters, whenever you face trials of many kinds, because you know that the testing of your faith produces perseverance. Let perseverance finish its work so that you may be mature and complete, not lacking anything (James 1:2-4, NIV).

Always Sunny

In northern Chile, between the Andes Mountains and the Pacific Ocean, lies a narrow strip of land where the sun shines almost every day.

Clouds seldom gather over the valley, and morning after morning, the sun rises over the tall mountains. Each day, it shines brightly overhead, and every evening, it brings a beautiful sunset.

Although storms can be seen in the distance, the sun continues to shine upon this strip of land.

One might imagine this area to be a paradise, but it is far from that. It is a barren and desolate wasteland. There are no streams of water, and nothing grows there.

We often long for total sunshine and continuous happiness in life. We do our best to avoid the heartaches and troubles. Like that sunny, unfertile part of Chile, life without clouds and even an occasional storm would not allow for growth. But even though storms do come, they will also end, and the sun will shine again.

There are no limits to caring ®

June 20

Oil and perfume make the heart glad, and the sweetness of a friend comes from his earnest counsel (Proverbs 27:9, ESV).

True Friends

Eleanor Roosevelt wrote, "Many people will walk in and out of your life, but only true friends will leave footprints in your heart".

Who is it that has left footprints in your heart? Is it a teacher that in-spired you to do your best, an employer who gave you a job or opportunity you thought you would never have, a parent who gave you the foundation that you needed, or a spouse who sticks with you no matter what?

They made a difference in who we have become. Do not wait until some-one is gone to express what a blessing they have been. Express it today.

Each day we have opportunities to leave footprints in the hearts of others by serving and caring. When we do, we demonstrate that there are no limits to caring.

There are no limits to caring ®

June 21

When there is a prophet among you, I the LORD, reveal myself to them in visons, I speak to them in dreams (Numbers 12:6, NIV).

"Selling Out" Your Dreams

Richard Elder wrote the book *If I Knew Then What I Know Now*. He asked hundreds of senior executives and leaders, "What do you know now that you wished someone had told you 25 years ago?" He found that the number one issue was that they did not follow their dreams.

A person who did follow his dreams was Ray Kroc, the founder of McDonalds's. A long-term employee said, "When Ray talked about McDonald's, he touched people, he moved them. By the time he got through talking about buns, you were hungry." This man did not sell out on his dream. His dream became a reality. Millions of people have benefited from his dream. Don't sell out on your dreams. Make them happen.

Remember there are no limits to your dreams. You too can have a Big Mac Day!

There are no limits to caring ®

June 22

I can do all things through him who strengthens me (Philippians 4:13, ESV).

Dreams-Jaws

Ted Hunter raced motorcycles and dreamed of one day being a professional racer. Then he had an accident and was blinded.

In an interview, he said, "I had a dream. When the accident happened, I had to think of new dreams. I had a moment of despair."

The interviewer asked, "a moment?" Hunter said, "Yes, about ten minutes, because I realized that for ages and ages, people have been blind, and there was going to be something good for me in this." And he ultimately created a product called "Jaws" which enables people who are blind to translate the written word from a computer.

Re-dream broken dreams—make a difference, regardless.

There are no limits to caring ®

June 23

For which of you, desiring to build a tower, does not first sit down and count the cost, whether he has enough to complete it?
(Luke 14:28, ESV).

Baby Leopard

In a small village in India, some children found an adorable kitten while they were outside playing. So, they brought it home to their mom and dad, begging them to let the kitten stay.

The next day they were playing when suddenly, their cute little kitten growled. It was then that the children realized the adorable animal was not a kitten, it was a leopard cub.

While kittens make great pets, leopards don't. The family decided to release the leopard cub back into the wild, near where they had found it the previous day.

Sometimes, new things can look pretty appealing: purchasing a shiny new car, remodeling your house, or even bringing home a cute new pet.

But then you realize the responsibility is more than you can handle. Know what you're getting into before you let the cat out of the bag.

There are no limits to caring ®

June 24

*Consider it pure joy, my brothers and sisters, whenever you face
trials of many kinds* (James 1:2, NIV).

Jesse Owens

Have you been watching the Olympics? Go back in history to
1936…Jesse Owens competed in the Olympics in the face of
racial discrimination.

He was born in 1913, in Alabama. He began running in high school
and joined the track team. As a senior in high school, Jesse tied the
world record in the 100-yard dash.

At a track meet in 1935, he set three world records. He had
accomplished what had never been done before. Jesse Owens
entered the 1936 Olympics, which were held in Nazi Germany.
Hitler was going to prove to the world that the German people were
the dominant race. Jesse had different plans, and that year, he
became the first American in the history of Olympic Track and
Field to win four gold medals.

Jesse Owens was the son of a sharecropper and grandson of a slave.
He overcame circumstances and won the gold. He showed that we
cannot let circumstances defeat us.

June 25

For all the promises of God find their Yes in him. That is why it is through him that we utter our Amen to God for his glory (2 Corinthians 1:20; ESV).

Blessings/Attitudes

A young man was graduating from college, and his wealthy father asked him what he wanted for a graduation present. The son asked his father for a new sports car, promising it was all he wanted. Graduation day arrived and his father presented him with a small box, telling him how proud he was.

The son opened the small box and was upset to find a Bible. "All of your money and this is it?" he screamed as he left, leaving the Bible.

Sometime later, he received word that his father had passed away. When he went to his father's house, he found the Bible still sitting where he'd left it so long ago. Thumbing through the pages, an envelope fell out. In it, a car key, with his graduation date and a car tag reading, "Paid in Full".

We always miss God's blessings when our attitudes are not right. Don't miss your blessings today.

There are no limits to caring ®

June 26

If one of you says to them, "Go in peace; keep warm and well fed," but does nothing about their physical needs, what good is it? (James 2:16, NIV).

Decision Time

I've got an old riddle for you. See if you can guess the answer. "Three frogs sat on a log and one decided to jump off. How many frogs were left on the log?"

Did you say, "TWO"? Sounds like good math. But the correct answer is "THREE." You see, just because the frog *decided* to jump off the log does not necessarily mean that it actually *did*!

Sometimes there is a gap between what we *decide* to do and what we *actually* do. Today would be a wonderful day to just go ahead and do some of those good things you have been saying you were going to do. Now is the time to do good. DO IT! Just DO IT! DO IT today.

There are no limits to caring ®

June 27

*So do not fear, for I am with you; do not be dismayed, for I am
your God. I will strengthen you and help you;
I will uphold you with my righteous right hand.*
(Isaiah 41:10, NIV).

Surprise

A group of expectant fathers were in a hospital waiting room,
waiting to hear news of their wives in the delivery room. A
nurse came in and announced to one man that his wife had just
given birth to twins.

"That's quite a coincidence" he laughed, "I play for the Minnesota
Twins!" A few minutes later, another nurse came in and announced
to another man that he was the father of triplets.

"That's amazing," he exclaimed, "I work for the 3M company." At
that point, a third man fell off his chair and laid down on the floor.

One of the new dads asked if he was feeling okay. "No," he replied,
"This is not good; I work for the 7-Up company."

We all receive unexpected news sometimes. Life throws us a
surprise from time to time. But whether it's 2, 3, or 7, God offers
us the grace and strength to deal with surprises.

There are no limits to caring ®

June 28

Behold, what I have seen to be good and fitting is to eat and drink and find enjoyment in all the toil with which one toils under the sun the few days of his life that God has given him, for this is his lot (Ecclesiastes 5:18, ESV).

Moments – Live Now!

Last night, I stopped by my son's room to tuck him in, make sure he was safe. Then I went by my daughter's room. She was almost asleep. Both so peacefully present...so secure in their family. But it wasn't last night, it just seems that way. It was 40 years ago.

Where did time go? When we were changing diapers, we thought those days would never end. But they did, and now the nest is empty.

Life is about change. And sometimes we live for the future, only to realize that when we get to the future, we want to live in the past. The key is learning to live here and now. Joy is for the moment, for now---not the future.

Find joy and happiness in the people about you---now...even in that son or daughter that you can no longer tuck in. Have a great day living in the moment!

There are no limits to caring ®

June 29

All these people died still believing what God had promised them.
They did not receive what was promised, but they saw it all from
a distance and welcomed it. They agreed that they were
foreigners and nomads here on
earth (Hebrews 11:13, NLT).

Abe Lincoln

Back in 1809, two old timers were leaning against an old rail fence. One asked the other, "What's going on in your neck of the woods?" "Not much; the Lincolns just had a baby boy."

Recently, when I came home from a trip to Arizona, I brought my daughter a beautiful, handmade pottery dish. Her response was, "I think this is one of those things that I just may appreciate after you die."

Sometimes, who we are now and the value of what we do now is not really seen until after we are long gone. Not in his day, but today, Lincoln is known as one of the greatest of all Presidents, and, I am sure one day, the pottery dish will become important to someone.

There are no limits to caring ®

June 30

The day of the LORD is near . . . As you have done, it will be done to you; your deeds will return upon your own head (Obadiah 1:15, NIV).

Kindness

Howard Kelly was a poor boy who sold goods from door to door. At one house in particular, he was very hungry and decided to ask for a glass of water. A young woman opened the door and, instead of water, she brought him a glass of milk. Howard asked, "How much do I owe you?" "You don't owe me anything," she replied.

Years later, that same woman became very ill. Specialists came to study her rare disease. Dr. Howard Kelly was one of them. He recognized her at once and, from that day on, he was determined to save her life. After a long struggle, she pulled through.

When Dr. Kelly reviewed her bill, he wrote something on the edge, then sent it to her room. When she opened the bill, she read these words..... "Paid in full with one glass of milk." Signed, Dr. Howard Kelly.

What you give always has a way of coming back again.

There are no limits to caring ®

July 1

Let love be your only debt, If you love others, you have done all that the Law demands (Romans 13:8, CEV).

Amateur

After a great fire leveled London in 1666, the royal architect, Sir Christopher Wren, faced the most challenging project - the rebuilding of St. Paul's Cathedral. He worked on it for thirty-five years! After personally escorting Queen Anne through the new cathedral, she reportedly turned to Wren and said, "It is awful, it is amusing, obviously the work of an amateur!"

Sir Christopher bowed deeply and offered profuse thanks to his Queen! Why? Because in the 18th century in England, a*wful* meant "filled with awe," *amusing* meant "amazing." The word *amateur*, coming from the Latin root, "amore," meant "one who did something for the love of it!" She had paid him the ultimate compliment.

To do something "for the love of it" is still the best one can do.

There are no limits to caring ®

July 2

He who withholds kindness from a friend forsakes the fear of the Almighty (Job 6:14, ESV).

Jackie Robinson

Jackie Robinson was the first African-American to play major league baseball. In his first season with the Brooklyn Dodgers, he faced hostility because of his race.
- Pitchers threw fast balls at his head.
- Mean words were shouted by the home crowds in Brooklyn.

During one game, Robinson committed an error. He stood at second base, humiliated, while the fans insulted him.

Another teammate called time-out, walked over to Robinson, and put his arm around his shoulder. As soon as he did, the fans grew silent.

Robinson later said, "That arm around my shoulder saved my career." Jackie Robinson went on to become one of baseball's all-time greats.

An arm around his shoulder made the difference.

Don't be afraid to offer an arm of support to someone today. After all, you never know what impact a simple act of kindness can make.

There are no limits to caring ®

July 3

And my God will supply every need of yours according to his riches in glory in Christ Jesus (Philippians 4:19, ESV).

Bridge

John Roebling, an engineer, had a dream to build a spectacular bridge connecting New York with Long Island. However, bridge experts said it couldn't be done.

But Roebling knew that it could be done. He and his son, Washington, hired a crew and began to build their bridge.

Only a few months underway, an accident took John Roebling's life. His son, Washington, took the lead on the project. A few years later, Washington became ill. He was unable to talk or barely move. Despite his tremendous disability, Washington had a burning desire to complete the bridge.

All he could do was move one finger. So, he developed a code of communication with his wife. For 13 years, he tapped out instructions with his finger until the bridge was completed.

Today the spectacular Brooklyn Bridge stands because of determination beyond circumstances. You can see that determination today in New York, or you can see it today in the lives of people with disabilities, who never give up.

July 4

Jesus said to the people who believed in him, "You are truly my disciples if you remain faithful to my teachings." And you will know the truth, and the truth will set you free (John 8:31-32, NLT).

The Declaration of Independence

Today, we celebrate the Declaration of Independence. It's about what our forefathers did for us. But it is really about the freedom that we experience every day.

Today is about what our military and our police are doing to protect us and to ensure our freedom. . .but freedom is not free. Those before us have paid the price for our freedom, and today, our sons and daughters are laying their lives on the line for our freedom.

At VOA, we too are helping individuals find freedom...
- Freedom from the chains of alcoholism or drugs
- Freedom from the chains of poverty
- Freedom from the chains of disabilities

We work to set people free...so they can learn to fish...for we know if we give them a fish, they are free for a day from hunger, but if we teach them to fish...they are free for a lifetime.

There are no limits to caring ®

July 5

Whoever walks with the wise becomes wise, but the companion of fools will suffer harm (Proverbs 13:20, ESV).

Make no friendship with a man given to anger, nor go with a wrathful man, lest you learn his ways and entangle yourself in a snare (Proverbs 22:24-25).

Friendship

Friends are very important. Without friends, life becomes very difficult, if not impossible.

A friend sticks closer than a brother. A friend is someone who helps you when you are down, one who celebrates with you when you are up. A friend is one you can count on through the difficult times and the good times. A friend is someone who knows you and likes you anyway. An ancient proverb says, "If you want a friend, be a friend."

Successful people surround themselves with the kind of friends they wish to emulate. If you want to soar like an eagle, don't stay in the barnyard with the chickens - chickens can't fly very high. Surround yourself with eagles. Find someone you want to be like and make a friend of that person.

There are no limits to caring ®

July 6

Keep your conduct among the Gentiles honorable, so that when they speak against you as evildoers, they may see your good deeds and glorify God on the day of visitation (1 Peter 2:12, ESV).

Music

Pippa Passes was a long poem written by Robert Browning. Pippa played a musical instrument. One day, he went by four homes and at each home, he played his music. He did not realize that at each home, there were people in crisis. And the music he played helped change people's lives. Pippa went on his way, playing his music, and he never knew he had just changed the course of a crisis.

When we express our music of joy and happiness, we always interrupt crises. People's lives are changed and made better because we played the music of love and kindness that makes all the difference. You may never know the good you have done. But just keep on doing good. It really matters.

There are no limits to caring ®

July 7

But Peter and John replied, "Which is right in God's eyes: to listen to you, or to him? You be the judges! (Acts 4:19, NIV).

Experts

Have you ever had those experts in your life tell you what you are not capable of achieving? After the well-known actor/dancer Fred Astaire's first screen test, a 1933 memo from the MGM testing director said, "Can't act, slightly bald, can dance – a little."

Experts said of the famous football coach Vince Lombardi, "He possesses minimal football knowledge and lacks motivation."

In middle school, the experts said that I would not be able to attend college. But I did. Heather Whitestone was told that her achievements would be very limited because she was deaf, but she became Miss Alabama and Miss America. Don't let the experts stop your dreams. Believe in yourself. Reach your dreams.

There are no limits to caring ®

July 8

I have fought the good fight, I have finished the race,
I have kept the faith (2 Timothy 4:7, ESV).

Two Types of Strength

Harold Phillips says, "There are two types of strength.

> There is the strength of the wind that sways the mighty oak, and there is the strength of the oak that withstands the power of the wind."

> There is the strength of the locomotive that pulls the heavy train across the bridge, and there is the strength of the bridge that holds up the weight of the train.

One is active strength, the other is passive strength.

One is the power to keep going, the other is the power to keep still.

One is the strength by which we overcome, the other is the strength by which we endure.

Some days we show our strength by holding on, some days by letting go.

My challenge is to know which strength to use and when! To know is wisdom!

There are no limits to caring ®

July 9

The Lord is my strength and my shield; in him my heart trusts,
and I am helped; my heart exults, and with my song I give thanks
to him (Psalm 28:7, ESV).

Fortunate

In 1982, Steven Callahan was crossing the Atlantic Ocean in his
sailboat when it sank. He drifted in his life raft, surviving on his
meager supplies and fish. He was hungry. He was thirsty. And he
was alone.

It seemed that every day, he faced a new difficulty. He braved the
rough waves and storms. When his life raft was punctured, he
bailed water night and day – exhausted from lack of food and sleep.

He was found 76 days later, malnourished and dehydrated – but
alive. Steven Callahan had managed to keep going when all hope
seemed lost.

Callahan later wrote about his ordeal, saying that the only way he
survived was by reminding himself that he was fortunate. When
all seemed hopeless, he refused to give up. He had learned not to
despair, no matter how bad the situation was.

When difficult times come, count your blessings. Be positive,
refuse to give up. See yourself as fortunate, blessed.

There are no limits to caring ®

July 10

People may be right in their own eyes, but the LORD examines their heart. (Proverbs 21:2, NIV).

Planting

One afternoon, a woman came upon a trap with a frog inside of it. The frog said to her, "If you release me from this trap, I will grant you three wishes." After the frog was freed, he said, "There is a condition to your wishes. Whatever you wish for, your husband will also get, multiplied by ten!"

For her first wish, the woman asked to be the most beautiful woman in the world. The frog reminded her, "This wish will make your husband the most handsome man in the world, and women will flock to him." The woman replied, "That's okay, because I will be the most beautiful woman, and he'll have eyes only for me."

For her second wish, she asked to be the richest woman in the world. The frog said, "Your husband will be ten times richer than you." The woman replied, "That's okay."

For her third wish, the woman said, "I'd like a mild heart attack...."

What would be your three wishes?

There are no limits to caring ®

July 11

For to me to live is Christ, and to die is gain (Philippians 1:21, ESV).

How to Die

Jennifer and Joe had been married for 26 faithful years when they learned that he had a brain tumor. He was given 6 months to live. He lived 15 months. After more than 30 years in their relationship, Joe died.

Jennifer later said, "My husband taught our three children much, but if he taught them nothing else, he taught them how to die." Joe accepted death and chose to make his last days positive and joyful.

When we learn how to die, we learn how to live. Each day, each moment, each family member, each friend becomes important for the moment. Do you know how to live? If you know how to die, then you know how to live – and make the most of every day.

There are no limits to caring ®

July 12

He will yet fill your mouth with laughter, ad your lips with shouts of joy (Job 8:21, NIV).

Younger Generation

Some words of wisdom from the younger generation:

Pat, age 10, offers, "Never trust a dog to watch your food."

Mike, 14, says, "When your dad is mad and asks you, "Do I look stupid?" don't answer him."

Mary, age 14, suggests "Never tell your mom her diet's not working."

Randy, 9, says, "Stay away from prunes."

Kay, 9, suggests, "Never hold a dust buster and a cat at the same time."

Joseph, 9, says, "You can't hide a piece of broccoli in a glass of milk."

Nancy, 15, offers this, "If you want a kitten, start out by asking for a horse."

Laura, 9, says, "Felt markers are not good to use as lipstick."

Ivy, 8, says, "Never try to baptize a cat."

This is a great day for laughing!

There are no limits to caring ®

July 13

But there's also this, it's not too late—God's personal Message!
— "Come back to me and really mean it!...!" Change your life,
not just your clothes. Come back to God, your God. And here's
why: God is kind and merciful. He takes a deep breath, puts up
with a lot. This most patient God, extravagant in love, always
ready to cancel catastrophe (Joel 2:12-13, MSG).

Change

A book title caught my eye: *IS IT TOO LATE TO RUN AWAY AND JOIN THE CIRCUS?* This book is about personal change.

It is never really too late to change. Some change is without choice. Perhaps the most significant changes are those related to choice.

It has been said, "Old dogs can't learn new tricks". That may be true of old dogs, but that is not true of you and me. We can learn new ways of living.

What do you want to spend the rest of your life doing? Just what you are doing today? If you want a change, what are you doing today to make it happen?

Today is the first day of the rest of your life. Make the most of it.

There are no limits to caring ®

July 14

For I will be merciful toward their iniquities and I will remember their sins no more (Hebrews 8:12, ESV).

Mistakes

A popular truism goes like this, "We all learn from our mistakes." But, is that true? The sad truth is that there are times when we do not learn from our mistakes. We often make the same errors over and over again.

Writer Michael Levine offers a practical suggestion: When you make a mistake, write down what you've learned before a week passes. The process of writing it and reading it can help you avoid repeating it.

That sounds like good advice. Why not try that this week? That is, if you make a mistake! It wouldn't hurt to go ahead and get pen and paper handy! My pen and paper are ready!

There are no limits to caring ®

July 15

*Today I am eighty-five years old. I am as strong now as I was
when Moses sent me on that journey, and I can still travel and
fight as well as I could then. So, give me the hill country that the
LORD promised me* (Joshua 14:10-12, NLT).

Age of Grandma

Visiting my grandmother in the nursing home when she was 92,
I asked, "Grandma are there any old people here?" She
thought a minute, "Yes, there is one 98 and another 96." For some
reason, she didn't include herself. To her, age is something in your
mind. If you don't mind, it doesn't matter.

How old would you be if you didn't know how old you are?
Whatever our age, it need not stop us from dreaming dreams and
making those dreams a reality. Whatever our age, we can reach
out to those about us with kindness and a helping hand. Whatever
our age, we can find ways to make our community a better place.

Just because we're over 30 is no excuse to sit on the sidelines.
Don't let numbers keep you from being all that you can be.

There are no limits to caring ®

July 16

A good name is to be chosen rather than great riches (Proverbs 22:1, ESV).

Good Name

What is your name? Your name probably is one of the most important things you have. A name can open doors that money can never move. Who you are, that's your name. You need to cherish it and protect it.

The way you live, the way you give and the way you care has everything to do with what your name is. In the Old Testament, the Proverbist wrote "A good name is to be more desired than great riches."

Create a good name by living a good life, by caring about others, by investing your time and resources in the lives of others. A good name is the one thing you can take with you and also leave behind. Cherish your name.

There are no limits to caring ®

210

July 17

Commit your way to the LORD; and he will act (Psalm 37:5, ESV).

Committed

Philip C. McGraw, in his book *Life Strategies*, offers the time-honored formula for taking purposeful action.

What this formula says is…BE committed, DO what it takes, and you will HAVE what you want.

Most of us know what we would like to have. Many of us are willing to do what it takes. But the foundational key is being committed.

Being willing to stay for the long haul, the long term, that's commitment. Without commitment to a job or to a relationship, we will fail. With commitment, we can have what we want. Stay committed.

There are no limits to caring ®

July 18

Do not judge, and you will not be judged. Do not condemn, and you will not be condemned. Forgive, and you will be forgiven (Luke 6:37, NIV).

Judge

A little girl watching her mother do the dishes at the kitchen sink suddenly noticed that her mother had several strands of white hair sticking out in contrast on her brunette hair. She asked, "Mom, why are some of your hairs white?" Her mother replied, "Well, every time that you do something wrong and make me cry or unhappy, one of my hairs turns white." The little girl thought about this revelation for a moment and then said, "Mom, how come all of Grandma's hairs are white?"

Strange how the way we judge other people seems to come back to us. Psychologists call it projection, but what people need is neither judgment, nor projection, nor an extra portion of guilt for stuff they didn't do. Why not see beauty in those about you and have no need to pass judgment?

July 19

*He died for everyone so that those who receive his new life will
no longer live for themselves. Instead, they will live for Christ,
who died and was raised for them* (2 Corinthians 5:15, NLT).

Unwanted

Mother Teresa said, "The biggest disease today is not leprosy
or tuberculosis, but rather the feeling of being unwanted."

If that's true, it constitutes both bad news and good news. Bad
news, in that it is universal, affecting millions of persons. Good
news, in that we can do something about this disease. People like
you and me could eradicate it by demonstrating care toward one
another.

A family member who needs to hear "I love you." A co-worker
who needs a pat on the back. The disabled and disenfranchised
who need an act of compassion. These opportunities are here and
now.

And if we feel unwanted, then by reaching out to another, we can
change that in a moment. The fact is we are ALL needed by
someone.

There are no limits to caring ®

July 20

For I decided to know nothing among you except Jesus Christ and him crucified (1 Corinthians 2:2, ESV).

Memory

A young parish minister about to deliver his first sermon asked a retired minister for advice on how to capture the congregation's attention. "Start with an opening line that's certain to grab them," the older man said. For example: 'Some of the best years of my life were spent in the arms of a woman who was not my wife.'" He smiled at the younger man's shocked expression before adding, "She was my mother."

The next Sunday, the young clergyman nervously stood in front of his congregation. Then he began, "Some of the best years of my life were spent in the arms of a woman who was not my wife."

He was pleased – he got their attention – then became panic-stricken. "But for the life of me, I can't remember who she was!"

Don't forget the important things in life.

There are no limits to caring ®

July 21

This is love: not that we loved God, but that he loved us and sent his Son as an atoning sacrifice for our sins (1 John 4:10, NIV).

Children on Love

Some children were asked, "What is falling in love like?" Roger, 9 responded, "It's like an avalanche, where you have to run for your life."

Leo, age 7, said, "If falling in love is anything like learning to spell, I don't want to do it. It takes too long."

Some other children offered opinions about love. Bobby, 8, said "Love will find you, even if you are trying to hide from it. I have been trying to hide from it since I was five, but the girls keep finding me."

Regina, 10, said, "I'm not rushing into being in love. I'm finding fourth grade hard enough."

Alonzo, 9, said, "Don't do things like have smelly, green sneakers. You might get a lot of attention, but attention ain't the same thing as love."

Seek to show the world the true meaning of love!

July 22

*Grandchildren are the crown of the aged, and the glory of a son
is his father.*
(Proverbs 17:6, BSB).

Levi

Do you know Levi Matthew Wilburn? I thought the world
would know him by now! I met him Sunday morning, July
22, 2007.... before sunrise.

You may have not heard of him. Or you may have met your own
Levi. But he changed my world. He was my first grandson! And
from the very first day, he found a special place in my heart. He
is more than I could imagine.

Who will he become?

His parents will have a profound impact on who he will become.
On that first day, I saw a mother giving unconditional love, a
father affirming his son, parents concerned about the details of
caring for a child.

Affirmation and unconditional love—qualities that build a
life...to become what God wants. Every child deserves a father
and mother. And even grandparents!

Levi will add a new load to the heart, but the heart will find a new
dimension to loving and living, even for this Papa.

Giving birth is love indeed, so is parenting.

There are no limits to caring ®

July 23

Through the praise of children and infants you have established a stronghold against your enemies, to silence the foe and the avenger (Psalm 8:2, NIV).

Children's Prayers

Listen to actual prayers from children:

~Dear God: Please send a new baby for Mommy. The new baby you sent last week cries too much.

~Dear God: Who did you make smarter? Boys or girls? My sister and I want to know.

~Dear God: How many angels are there in heaven? I would like to be the first kid in my class to know the answer.

~Dear God: Could you please give my brother some brains? So far, he doesn't have any.

~Dear Lord: Thank you for the nice day today. You even fooled the TV weather man.

~Dear God: Please help me in school. I don't need help in anything else.

~Dear God: Do you have any helpers in Heaven? I would like to be one of Your helpers in Heaven during summer vacation.

~Dear God: I need a raise in my allowance. Could you have one of your angels tell my father?

The honesty of children is refreshing.

There are no limits to caring ®

July 24

Like a city whose walls are broken through is a person who lacks self-control
(Proverbs 25:28, NIV).

Self-Control

One day, when our granddaughter Kayden was four years old, I was the only family member that was able to attend one of her school events. I was excited! That morning, as I was leaving home, I slipped three small pieces of her favorite candy in my pocket.

After the event, she ran up and hugged me. I slipped the three pieces of candy out of my pocket and said, "Here…I brought you a surprise." She looked at the candy in my hand without touching it and said, "I can't eat candy now."

Wow! That's self-control! At four years old, as much as she wanted the candy, she said no. Imagine if we all had that kind of self-control… wouldn't the world be a better place, and wouldn't we be better people? Proverbs 25:28 says, "Like a city whose walls are broken down is a man who lacks self-control." Practice self-control. It will improve your life!

There are no limits to caring ®

July 25

Oh, the depth of the riches and wisdom and knowledge of God!
How unsearchable are his judgments and how inscrutable his
ways! (Romans 11:33, ESV).

Explanation

Attending a wedding for the first time, a little girl whispered to her mother, "Why is the bride dressed in white?" "Because white is the color of happiness, and today is the happiest day of her life," the mother tried to explain, keeping it simple.

The child thought about this for a minute, then said, "So why is the groom wearing black?"

Some things are hard to explain. Not only do they not add up in a child's mind, all of us have difficulty making sense of some things in life.

The good news is that we do not have to have an explanation for everything. Most of us would be hard pressed to give a scientific explanation for the formation of a rainbow, but that doesn't keep us from enjoying its beauty!

Have a beautiful day.

There are no limits to caring ®

July 26

Who is this uncircumcised Philistine that he should defy the armies of the living God? (1 Samuel 17:26, NIV).

Perspective

We have all heard, "It's all in how you look at it." The truth in that statement has to do with perspective. It's true as the poet says, "Two men looked through prison bars; one saw mud; the other, stars." The way we look at things in life makes all the difference.

In the biblical story of David and the giant, David's companions tried to discourage him. Their words to him were, "Goliath is so big, how can you expect to win?" David's perspective was different. "He's so big, how can I miss?"

It's all in how you look at it. Today is so big you can't help but have many opportunities to have fun, do good, and make a big hit.

There are no limits to caring ®

July 27

*O Jerusalem, Jerusalem, the city that kills the prophets and
stones those who are sent to it! How often would I have gathered
your children together as a hen gathers her brood under her
wings, and you were not willing!* (Luke 13:34, ESV).

God's Wings

After a forest fire in Yellowstone National Park, a ranger found
a bird literally petrified in ashes at the base of a tree.
Somewhat sickened by the eerie sight, he knocked over the bird
with a stick.

When he gently struck it, three tiny chicks came from under their
dead mother's wings. The loving mother, keenly aware of
impending disaster, had carried her offspring to the base of the tree
and had gathered them under her wings. When the blaze had
arrived and the heat had scorched her small body, the mother had
remained steadfast.

Because she was willing to give her all, those under her wings
would live. That's really what being a mother or a father is all
about. We have so much to learn from Mother Nature. What a
challenge!

There are no limits to caring ®

July 28

Teach us to use wisely all the time we have (Psalm 90:12, CEV).

Time

Is time management a problem for you? Do you have trouble getting a "handle" on the use of time? Someone told me, "Time is a phenomenon that keeps everything from happening at once."

Earl Nightingale had a good perspective when he said, "Don't let the fear of the time that it will take to accomplish something stand in the way of your doing it. The time will pass anyway; we might just as well put that passing time to the best possible use."

Perhaps it is best to think of time as a tool. Each day has 24 hours, and we usually have some choices as to how we will use them. Invest time today doing something that will make a positive difference in someone's life. We may not finish, but we can get started.

There are no limits to caring ®

July 29

*Commit your work to the LORD, and your plans will be
established* (Proverbs 16:3, ESV).

Success

When do you know you have been successful? When you have a paycheck and a 6-pack on a Friday night? Maybe, maybe not.

Ralph Waldo Emerson defined success: "to laugh often and much; to win the respect of intelligent people and the affection of children; to earn the appreciation of honest critics and to endure the betrayal of false friends; to appreciate beauty; to find the best in others; to leave the world a bit better whether by a healthy child, a garden patch, or a redeemed social condition; to know even one life has breathed easier because you have lived."

To me, he defined true success. Making a difference here and now. Leaving our world a better place to live, and enjoying the process.

There are no limits to caring ®

July 30

So, they are no longer two, but one flesh. Therefore, what God has joined together, let no one separate (Matthew 19:6, NIV).

Promises

People will sometimes ask a minister who has just performed a marriage ceremony, "Did you tie the knot good and tight?"

A minister friend of mine recently performed a wedding, in which he took a sash and literally bound together the wrists of the couple and then invited them to exchange their vows. Later, he told them, "The knot I tied with the sash is symbolic. The real knot that will bind you together is the keeping of the vows you just made. They are promises and will be as binding as you make them day by day."

No one can keep our promises for us. Sometimes promises are broken. Sometimes they need renewing. It has been said, "A promise made is a debt unpaid."

This could be a good day for renewing promises...for paying debts. Have a great day renewing promises.

There are no limits to caring ®

July 31

Nothing brings me greater happiness than to hear that my children are obeying the truth (3 John 1: 4, CEV).

Empty Nest

In one episode of the Andy Griffith Show, Opie, with his sling shot, accidentally shot a mother bird. He was saddened and wanted to provide food for the three baby birds. So, he put them in a cage and fed them worms every day.

When the birds became grown, his Dad suggested, "Opie, you may want to turn them loose." Somewhat reluctantly, Opie took each bird in his hand and said, "I've tried to raise you right, now fly!" And each bird flew, leaving an empty cage. His Dad said, "You know the cage is empty, but the trees are fuller."

Hodding Carter, Jr. said, "There are two lasting bequests we can give our children. One is roots, the other is wings." That's the challenge, and then there is the challenge of the empty nest. What then?

As parents, we are forever adjusting, stretching and growing as our nest changes. And for our offspring, we let them go, trusting God's Hand. If His Hand is not big enough, neither is ours!

There are no limits to caring ®

August 1

For I know the plans I have for you," declares the Lord, "plans to prosper you and not to harm you, plans to give you hope and a future" (Jeremiah 29:11, NIV).

Back to School

Summer is quickly ending, and students will be going back to school, college, or even graduate school. But many won't have a clue as to what they are doing... no direction for their lives. They wander aimlessly with no purpose.

However, other students will know that there is a plan for their lives, and they will live it out. Those are the people that have a direction and a sense of purpose. They have a mission in life.

How do you arrive at that point? Surrender yourself to God's hand ... He has a purpose for your life, and He will show it to you daily!

As David, the author of Psalms, pleaded to God, "Direct me in your path, for there I find delight." Find your delight in God's path for your life. And you will find joy in living.

There are no limits to caring ®

August 2

Walk in wisdom toward outsiders, making the best use of the time (Colossians 4:5, ESV).

Wasting Time

Do you ever feel like you're wasting time – never getting your to-do list done – always getting behind?

On her first day of school, a little girl came home, telling her mother how her first day had been a waste. "I'm wasting my time," she said to her mother. "I can't read, I can't write, and they won't let me talk." Some days are just a waste of time.

However, if you are reaching out in kindness to someone, that's not a waste of time. If you are expressing love to an elderly person, that's not a waste of time. If you're giving your child love, attention and validation, that's not a waste of time.

Today is a great day to stop your rush, evaluate how much time you waste - how much time you spend on the things that really count!

One thing is for sure, when you are caring for another, that's not a waste.

Love your neighbor! That's no waste of time!

There are no limits to caring ®

August 3

Dear children, let us not love with words or speech
but with actions and in truth. (1 John 3:18, NIV).

Wordless

A schoolteacher injured his back and had to wear a plaster cast around the upper part of his body. It was under his shirt and was not noticeable.

On the first day of school, still with the cast under his shirt, he found himself assigned to the toughest students in the school. Walking confidently into the rowdy classroom, he opened the window as wide as possible and sat at his desk. When a strong breeze made his tie flap, he took the stapler off his desk and stapled the tie to his chest.

Would you believe that discipline was not a problem from that day forward? As they say, perception is everything. There are times when we communicate most effectively without words. Our actions speak loudly. It is important that what we are doing is creative and positive. To wish a person well is fine, but to actually enable someone to improve their lot in life, is better.

There are no limits to caring ®

August 4

In his grace, God has given us different gifts for doing things well
(Romans 12:6, NLT).

What You Do Best

A little boy was talking to himself as he walked through his backyard, wearing his baseball cap, carrying a ball and bat. "I'm the greatest hitter in the world," he said. Then, he tossed the ball into the air, swung at it, and missed.

"Strike one!" he yelled. He picked up the ball, said again, "I'm the greatest hitter in the world!" He tossed the ball into the air, swung and missed. "Strike two!" he yelled.

He straightened his cap, said once more, "I'm the greatest hitter in the world!" tossed the ball, swung and missed.

"Strike three!" Then he said, "Wow! I'm the greatest pitcher in the world!"

What a perspective! It's called turning our liabilities into assets. We are not all meant to be home-run kings. Some of us have to pitch the ball. Find what you do best, and major on that. You may be the best in the world.

August 5

*Have mercy on me, O God, according to your unfailing love;
according to your great compassion blot out my transgressions*
(Psalms 51:1, NIV).

A Great Fall

Humpty Dumpty sat on a wall. Humpty Dumpty had a great fall. All the King's horses and all the King's men couldn't put Humpty together again.

When you have had your great fall, what then? Do you turn to your faith in God, to friends, to family to help put you together again?

Sometimes when we are really down, God may be doing more than we know. Often, there is that friend or family member wanting to reach out and to give a helping hand.

When life falls apart, don't run from people or your faith in God. Embrace both and discover help. When you come back, you will see other people who, too, have experienced a great fall, and now you can help that person rebuild.

Make it a great day...even when you have fallen apart.

August 6

Why am I discouraged? Why am I restless? I trust you! And I will praise you again because you help me, and you are my God (Psalm 43:5, CEV).

Snakes/Tolerance

We were sitting on our back porch, when a cottonmouth moccasin came sliding through our backyard and suddenly stopped. My wife got her gun, stood on the back steps, and blew his head off. One preemptive shot, a powerful gun, a great marksman, a dead snake.

A cottonmouth can kill you. It could kill a pet or child. We knew that he presented a clear and present danger to our household. We had all played where he was playing. We didn't call a neighborhood watch or the county commissioners to get their advice or approval.

I guess you could call it a unilateral action—or pre-emptive, or even reactive. The cottonmouth would have preferred tolerance. But not in my backyard.

We, as parents, have a responsibility to take unilateral pre-emptive actions to protect our kids from alcohol, drugs, pornography, gambling and the wrong crowd. Some tolerance destroys families and nations.

There are no limits to caring ®

August 7

Wisdom is like having two good eyes; foolishness leaves you in the dark (Ecclesiastes 2:14, CEV).

Shake It Off

A mule fell into a farmer's well. After carefully assessing the situation, the farmer decided that the mule wasn't worth saving. He enlisted his neighbors to help haul dirt to bury the old mule in the well.

The old mule was hysterical! But as the dirt hit his back, it suddenly dawned on the mule that every time a shovel of dirt landed on his back, he should shake it off and step up!

"Shake it off and step up…shake it off and step up," he repeated to encourage himself. Soon the old mule, battered and exhausted, stepped out of the well. What seemed would bury him actually blessed him…all because of the way he handled his adversity.

Some events in our lives, we must simply shake off – build upon them and go on. Shake it off and have a great day!

There are no limits to caring ®

August 8

So, God created mankind in his own image, in the image of God
he created them; male and female he created them.
(Matthew 6:20-21, ESV).

Value

We've all seen the stock market plummet. We look at the decline and say, "My value has gone down. I'm not worth what I used to be." Really? Is your value tied to the stock market? Are you really just worth what the stock market says? I don't think so. You're not.

God created you with value. He created you in His image. That image never goes down in value, no matter what happens to the economy. Your portfolio may look different, but your value never changes.

Perhaps, as you've had the opportunity to spend time in solitude… you've reflected on your value as God's creation. Maybe you've spent some good quality time with your family, your friends or neighbors. The value, suddenly seen in the importance of family and friends, has skyrocketed.

Sometimes when things go down, other things go up, such as the value we place on one another. What lessons have you learned during this time?

There are no limits to caring ®

August 9

If anyone has material possessions and sees a brother or sister in need but has no pity on them, how can the love of God be in that person? (1 John 3:17, NIV).

Happiest People

Noted educator Booker T. Washington said, "I began learning long ago that those who are happiest are those who do the most for others."

Truly those who have learned the value of giving have found the secret of happiness. "It is more blessed to give than to receive." While some may know how to say those words, few have found the power that those words unlock.

Well-known Mother Theresa found happiness and joy in the most difficult of situations --- by giving to those who had nothing. Others, who remain unknown, are quietly giving wherever they are. They have discovered the joy of giving --- and that has translated into the joy of living.

Our lives really begin to take on a new meaning, a richer purpose, when we experience doing for other people.

Make it a great day by doing for others.

There are no limits to caring ®

August 10

*Out of the mouths of babies and infants, you have established
strength because of your foes* (Psalms 8:2, ESV).

Outward Appearance

Students in my sister's 5-year old kindergarten class were in a
discussion about the age of their teacher. One student said,
"She's at least 80!" Another said, "No, no! She's 38!" And finally,
another student said, "Mrs. Griffin is not old. She just looks old!"
Out of the mouths of babes, sometimes, come great truths.

We can't always tell about a person just by the outward
appearance. Only after time with someone, do we really begin to
know who that person is.

Maybe we are better served not to make quick judgments about a
person until first we spend time getting to know that person. It's
not the outward gray hair that counts; it's the inner character--
that's what really matters.

August 11

Not one word of all the good promises that the LORD had made to the house of Israel had failed: all came to pass (Joshua 21:45, ESV).

Keeping Promises

Back in the mid-fifties, a five-year-old boy had an old wagon that had been discarded. The wagon however did not have a handle for pulling. A gentleman down the street told the young lad that he would get him a wagon handle from the junk yard. Every day, the young boy stood out in his yard, waiting for the man to walk home with a handle for the wagon.

The man never came home with the wagon handle. But every day, the boy believed this would be the day. It never happened.

When you make a promise, keep it. Some five-year-old boy may be counting on you to deliver what you promised. By the way, I was that boy.

Make today a great day by keeping promises.

August 12

Not by the way of eye-service, as people pleasers, but as servants of Christ, doing the will of God from the heart (Ephesians 6:6, ESV).

Perception

For weeks, a six-year-old lad kept telling his first-grade teacher about the baby brother or sister that was expected at his house. One day, the mother allowed the boy to feel the movements of the unborn child in her womb. The six-year old was obviously impressed, but he made no comment. He stopped talking to his teacher about it. Finally, the teacher said, "Tommy, whatever has become of that baby brother or sister you were expecting?" Tommy burst into tears and confessed, "I think Mommy ate it!"

The perception of children sometimes is humorous – maybe a little shocking. But adults, too, sometimes have the wrong perception about life. Happiness is not about getting, but giving; not about wealth, but about how one uses wealth for others; not about freedom from stress, but how we manage stress. Strange – how we see things. Maybe we just need a second look.

August 13

When others are happy, be happy with them, and when they are sad, be sad (Romans 12:15, CEV).

A Little Boy

A man was asked to judge a contest to find the child who cared the most. The winner was a four-year-old, whose next-door neighbor was an elderly man who had recently lost his wife.

When the little boy saw the man crying, he went into his yard, climbed onto his lap, and just sat there. His mother asked him what he said to the neighbor. The little boy said, "Nothing, I just helped him cry."

What a message! Sometimes, people just need us to help them cry. People don't need our wisdom or advice…they just need us—just to be there. To cry with them or maybe laugh with them. And we learned all this from a four-year-old who knew how to care.

There are no limits to caring ®

August 14

I praise you because I am fearfully and wonderfully made; your works are wonderful, I know that full well (Psalm 139:14, NIV).

Sunday School

A Sunday school teacher asked her children, "And why is it necessary to be quiet in church?" One bright little girl replied, "Because people are sleeping."

Another Sunday School class was studying the Ten Commandments. They were ready to discuss the last one. The teacher asked if anyone could tell her what it was. Susie raised her hand, stood tall, and quoted, "Thou shall not take the covers off the neighbor's wife."

A little boy was overheard praying: "Lord, if you can't make me a better boy, don't worry about it. I'm having a real good time like I am."

You know, we are each made unique and beautiful in our own way – God has not finished with any of us – he wants to make us better and to have lots of fun. The two go together.

August 15

So, whether you eat or drink or whatever you do,
do it all for the glory of God. (1 Corinthians 10:31, NLT).

Statue of Liberty

In his book *Lyrics*, Oscar Hammerstein tells of a picture of the Statue of Liberty on the cover of the New York *Herald Tribune* Sunday magazine. The picture had been taken from a helicopter, and it showed the top of the statue's head.

What was amazing was the detail that the artist had sculpted on the top of the statue's head. He must have been pretty sure that no one would ever see the top of the head, and he surely could not have known that anyone would one day fly over the statue.

But the artist had finished this part of the statue with as much care as he had devoted to the rest of the statue.

In all that you do, do your best and with great care. Pay attention to the details and take pride in your finished product. You never know when someone may fly over and see your work in detail.

August 16

As each has received a gift, use it to serve one another, as good stewards of God's varied grace (1 Peter 4:10, ESV).

Coffee

Tom and his wife Susan were having an argument about who should brew the coffee each morning. Susan explained to Tom that he should make the coffee because he wakes up first. That way, they wouldn't have to wait as long to get their coffee.

Tom explained to Susan that she is in charge of the cooking and makes better-tasting coffee anyway. "Besides," Tom said, "I can wait for my coffee."

Susan thought for a moment and then said, "No, you really should make the coffee. Besides, it's in the Bible that the man should brew the coffee."

Unbelieving, Tom asked Susan to show him, so she fetched the Bible, and opened it up to a book titled, "Hebrews."

Although you can twist the Bible to say almost anything, it is clear that service, serving one another, is the best way to ensure a happy marriage. Learn to serve first. Don't wait for someone else to fill your cup.

There are no limits to caring ®

August 17

*Love is patient and kind; love does not envy or boast; it is not
arrogant or rude. It does not insist on its own way; it is not
irritable or resentful; it does not rejoice at wrongdoing, but
rejoices with the truth. Love bears all things, believes all things,
hopes all things, endures all things.
Love never ends* (1 Corinthians 13:4-8, ESV).

Love at First Sight

I've been asked the question, "Do you believe in love at first
sight?" My response was, "Do you believe in love after many
sights?" The young couple who has a new baby, loves the baby at
first sight and believes it is so beautiful. But the real question is do
you believe in love after many sights of dirty diapers and midnight
feedings?

Love is more about the long haul than the first glance. The couple
who has been married for 50 years knows much more about love
than the couple who has been married for 50 minutes. The test of
true love is how you respond after that relationship has had many
sights, many challenges, many experiences. Love is for better or
for worse, not for a quick glance.

Love is about commitment, about roots, about eternal values.

242

August 18

For you are a people holy to the LORD your God. The LORD
your God has chosen you out of all the peoples on the face of the
earth to be his people, his treasured possession.
(Deuteronomy 7:6, NIV).

Value

A professor collected old and very rare books. One afternoon, while talking with his neighbor, he mentioned his passion for rare books. His neighbor told him that he had just thrown away a Bible that had been stored in his attic for years.

"I couldn't read it," the neighbor explained. "Someone named Gutenberg had printed it." "Not Gutenberg!" the professor exclaimed in horror. "The Gutenberg Bible was one of the first books ever printed. A copy just sold for several million dollars!"

His neighbor was surprised but then reassured the professor saying, "Well, mine probably wasn't worth anything. Some guy named Martin Luther had written all over it in German."

In today's economic times, things often lose their value. But some things never lose their value, like our loved ones, our family and friends. Treat them with care and importance for they are truly priceless.

There are no limits to caring ®

August 19

Don't you have a saying, "It's still four months until the harvest?" I tell you, open your eyes and look at the fields! They are ripe for harvest (John 4:35, NIV).

Sneeze

I bet you didn't know that you cannot sneeze with your eyes open. If you don't believe it, just try it the next time you feel a good sneeze coming on. Keep your eyes open.

Sneezing is one thing you can do when your eyes are closed. Other things cannot be done with eyes closed. When your eyes are closed, you don't see the people about you – the small child who needs a kiss - the old man who needs a hug – the young adolescent who needs a pat on the back.

When your eyes are closed…but you know it's really not about not seeing when your eyes are closed, for some who are blind are able to see those whose heart needs a touch. Whether your eyes are open or closed, reach out in love to one another.

There are no limits to caring ®

August 20

Let us think of ways to motivate one another to acts of love and good works (Hebrews 10:24, NLT).

Encouraging Words

Everyone needs an encouraging word. Do you remember the last time someone complimented you or offered a word of encouragement? Remember how good it felt? Look around today and find those who need an encouraging word from you. A co-worker, a spouse, a child, a salesclerk, or the waiter or waitress serving you.

By the way, I just saw a list of the 98 most encouraging words and expressions.

Excellent! Great job! Keep up the good work! Congratulations! Way to go! Nice work! You can do it! Outstanding! I like the way you work! You are a winner! You are the best! Exceptional performance! Keep looking up! You make my day! I'm proud of you!

Today, you will bump into people who need a word of encouragement from you. It won't cost you anything, but those who receive it will be richer and so will you.

There are no limits to caring ®

August 21

Hear, my son [child], your father's instruction, and forsake not your mother's teaching, for they are a graceful garland for your head and pendants for you neck (Proverbs 1:8-6, ESV).

Teaching our Kids

What are we teaching our children? You might be surprised!

My daughter stated in a university psychology research paper that her dad had taught her two things about how to drive: (1) Come to a complete stop at all stop signs. (2) How to drive with her knees.

I can remember teaching her about the stop signs, but for the life of me, I don't remember the part about driving with the knees! That would be irresponsible!

Well, maybe occasionally, I might have driven with my knees under some kind of emergency, but I certainly never intended to teach my daughter to do that!

Isn't it strange how what we do speaks louder than what we say? I wish I could have been more selective in what I taught my kids. They might have been a little better. But they learned from what they heard and what they saw. Now, don't be driving with your knees or texting.

There are no limits to caring ®

August 22

Do you not know that your bodies are the temples of the Holy Spirit whom you have received from God? You are not your own; you were bought at a price. Therefore, honor God with your bodies (1 Corinthians 6:19-20, NIV).

Take Care of Body

Adolph Zukor, a film producer, lived to be 103 years old. On his 100th birthday, he said, "If I knew I was going to live this long, I'd have taken better care of myself."

What happens if you live to be 100 or 80? Will you have taken care of your body well enough for the long haul? Is exercise a regular part of your daily activity? Do you eat healthy – did you skip breakfast or consume lots of sugar. The list could go on and on. Oh yes, what about stress? How do you handle your stress? Stress in traffic? Or how about ways to relax at work or after work. Oh well, you get the point – you might just end up with the same problem as Zukor.

Plan now and have a great body on your 100th birthday. You'll need it.

There are no limits to caring ®

August 23

Let no corrupting talk come out of your mouths, but only such as is good for building up, as fits the occasion, that it may give grace to those who hear (Ephesians 4:29, ESV).

Compliment

Mark Twain said, "I can live for two months on a compliment." It is amazing how a compliment encourages us to do our best and be our best.

A ten-year-old boy in nineteenth century London had a difficult life. His father was in debtor's jail, and the boy slept in an attic and took a job pasting labels on bottles in a grim, rat-infested warehouse.

He dreamed of becoming a writer. He sneaked out in the dead of night to mail his first manuscript. Story after story was rejected, until finally one was accepted. There was no pay, but he did receive a compliment and encouragement from the editor.

The compliment changed his life. Had it not been for that encouragement, he might have spent his entire life in a rat-infested factory.

Later, his books would bring about reforms in the treatment of children and the poor. He was Charles Dickens, author of *A Christmas Carol*.

There are no limits to caring ®

August 24

"Do two walk together, unless they have agreed to meet?"
(Amos **3:3 ESV**).

Cooperation

Two riders were on a two-man bicycle when they came to a steep hill. They both agreed to continue up the hill. The climb was difficult and they struggled to ascend the steep hill. After a terrific amount of effort, they finally made it to the top.

The front man, sweating profusely and breathing hard, turned back to his companion to say, "Boy that sure was a hard climb."

The other guy responded, "It sure was, and if I had not kept the brakes on we would have certainly rolled back down the hill."

Some want to make it to the top. Others just want to keep from going backwards.

I want to go to the top. I don't want to live in fear of going backwards.

Like in a marriage, in our jobs, in ALL of our relationships we have to pedal together at the same time if we want to move forward.

Don't brake when you need to be pedaling!!

There are no limits to caring ®

August 25

Forget the former things; do not dwell on the past (Isaiah 43:18, NIV).

New Leaf

I am sure you have heard the expression "turn over a new leaf." Did you ever wonder where this expression comes from? Believe it or not, it has nothing to do with leaves from a tree.

The expression actually refers to the "leaves" or pages in a book. It is talking about turning to a blank page where you can start with a clean slate…a new beginning.

Sometimes in life, we feel as though we are in a rut and can't get past a hard challenge or move beyond our mistakes.

You may need to turn over a new leaf with your spouse, or your boss, or a child. Turn the page. Start fresh with a blank page and new hope.

You may want to consult a friend or a spiritual leader on how best to turn over a new leaf.

Turning over a new leaf is a great way to start a new school year.

There are no limits to caring ®

August 26

Give instruction to a wise man, and he will be still wiser; teach a righteous man, and he will increase in learning (Proverbs 9:9, ESV).

School

School is back in session. The buses are running! Carpools are moving! The hectic pace has begun.

Susan came home from her first day of kindergarten. Her mother asked, "Well what did you learn today?" "Not enough I guess…they want me to come back tomorrow."

We just can't learn everything in a day. Like:
- How to be the best parent or
- How to go the extra mile or
- How to forgive

This kind of learning is not for a day, but for a lifetime. Even those in the Olympics are learning new lessons every day, like how to overcome a defeat of a lifelong dream or how to celebrate a victory without being obnoxious. Some of these things we did learn on our first day of kindergarten, but it takes a lifetime of practice.

There are no limits to caring ®

August 27

Do not be misled: Bad company corrupts good character
(1 Corinthians 15:33, NIV).

Flavor

So much of life's lessons are caught, rather than taught. It is believed that 89% of what we learn, we learn visually…that is, by watching others!

We tend to absorb the character of the people we admire. If we admire negative, skeptical people, we become skeptics. If we admire and spend time with optimistic people, we become optimistic. If we spend time with loving and devoted people, we tend to become more loving and devoted ourselves.

Someone put it this way: We take on the *flavor* of those who frequently touch us in our day-to-day existence. That being the case, who is "flavoring" your life? If you are dissatisfied with your flavor and want to change, then hook up with those people whose flavor you admire and desire. And remember, you are a flavoring influence yourself. Why not try to leave a good *flavor* in someone's life today!

August 28

I discipline my body like an athlete, training it to do what it should. Otherwise, I fear that after preaching to others I myself might be disqualified (1 Corinthians 9:27, NLT).

Exercise

In the last decade or so, Americans have become more conscious of the need to exercise, particularly exercise to benefit the heart. It has become very obvious that regular physical exercise is really important for our physical, emotional, and spiritual health. People are going to gyms, using exercise equipment at home, and employing personal trainers.

Walking is my exercise of choice. Others jog or run. Find what's best for you, and just do it! Your body needs it.

John Andrew Holmes made the following statement about exercise. "There is no exercise better for the heart than reaching down and lifting people up." He's right. Lifting people up is heart exercise. And, the more reaching you do, the stronger your heart becomes.

An exercise of the heart makes our community a better place to live. It also makes you a stronger and healthier person. Make it a great day, reaching and uplifting.

August 29

This is what the Scriptures mean when they say, "No eye has seen, no ear has heard, and no mind has imagined what God has prepared for those who love him" (1 Corinthians 2:9, NLT).

The Fork

A minister was visiting an elderly lady with a terminal illness. She told him how she wanted her funeral to be conducted. Then she told the minister that she wanted to be buried with a fork in her hand.

When the minister asked why, she said, "As a child, after dinner, Mama would collect the plates and tell us, 'Save your forks.' That would let us know dessert was coming."

"After people view my remains, they'll want to know about that fork. You tell 'em that was my way of saying, "Hold on to your forks, the best is yet to come!"

That kind of faith represents a healthy regard for the future. Has your best already been? Are you doing those things such as investing in the lives of others, which will ensure that the rest of your life can be the best?

Don't throw away your fork before it's over! The best is yet to come!

August 30

For by grace you have been saved through faith. And this is not your own doing; it is the gift of God, not a result of works, so that no one may boast (Ephesians 2:8-9, ESV).

Amazing Grace

In 1725, a boy was born into a devout Christian family. Orphaned at the age of 7, his new guardians made him disavow his faith. Miserable and rebellious, he ran away to sea. His wild nature brought him many adventures and narrow escapes. When he was locked up on an African, slave-trading ship for drunken behavior, he reflected on his childhood experience. Then, when the ship came close to sinking in a violent storm, he experienced a spiritual awakening.

Two years later, he was ordained as a minister and went on to write over 100 hymns. We remember John Newton for his hymn *Amazing Grace*.

No matter how severe the storms or the circumstances of life in which we find ourselves, change for the better is possible. Amazing good news for John Newton. Good news for us, as well.

There are no limits to caring ®

August 31

*I planted the seeds, Apollos watered them, but God made them
sprout and grow* (1 Corinthians 3:6, CEV).

Eyes on the Prize

Growing Chinese bamboo requires patience, perseverance, and a large investment of time and labor. For the first year after planting, it is watered and fertilized every day. At the end of that year, the plant has grown to six inches. For the next five years, the plant is watered and fertilized daily. At the end of the fifth year, the plant is still only six inches tall! However, in the next five weeks, it will grow to the tremendous height of 90 feet!

During those first five years, the plant was developing the root structure required to support it. The planters knew that an investment of five years would produce a great prize.

The better things in life require more time and effort. Friendships, marriage, job skills. Those who are most successful keep their eyes on the goal and make the investment of time, knowing the reward will be worth it.

There are no limits to caring ®

September 1

Suppose one of you wants to build a tower. Won't you first sit down and estimate the cost to see if you have enough money to complete it? (Luke 14:29, NIV).

$10 is $10

Every year, Stumpy and Martha would go to the state fair, and Stumpy would say he wanted to ride in the airplane. Martha would always say, "That ride costs $10, and $10 is $10!" This year Stumpy said, "I'm 71. If I don't ride it now, I may never get another chance." Martha replied, "Stumpy, that ride costs $10, and $10 is $10."

The pilot, hearing the conversation, offered them a deal. He said, "I will ride you both for free, if you can stay quiet for the entire ride. If you say one word, it's full price." They agreed, and up they went. The pilot did all his twists, turns, and rolls, trying to rattle them. Not one word. Finally, he landed and said, "I did everything I could to get you to yell out, but you didn't."

Stumpy replied, "Well, I was gonna say something when Martha fell out, but $10 is $10."

In life, it is always important to consider the cost!

There are no limits to caring ®

September 2

Above all else, guard your heart, for everything you do flows from it.(Proverbs 4:23, NIV).

Wishes

Three men were in a life boat. Their situation was getting hopeless. No food. No water. Getting weaker by the hour. Then, one of them saw a bottle floating by. He opened the bottle, and a genie popped out!

"I'll grant each of you a single wish," the genie said. "I wish I was home," said the first man. And, poof, he disappeared.

"I wish I was home too," said the second man. Then, poof, he disappeared also.

The third man looked around and saw his friends gone. "Gee, I'm kind of lonely," he said. "I wish I had my friends back here with me."

The old adage is that we should "Be careful what we wish for." Wishes, like dreams, do sometimes come true.

What do you wish for? More stuff? A better world? A new you? Your wishes and dreams say a great deal about you. Self-centered, or centered on others.

There are no limits to caring ®

September 3

*"If you keep knocking long enough, he will get up and give you
whatever you need because of your . . . persistence"*
(Luke 11:8, NTL).

Goodyear

In the 1830's, rubber was in high demand. Everybody wanted
rubber, and factories sprang up to meet the demand. But, the
rubber was messy. It froze in winter and turned glue-like in
summer.

Not one of the factories survived, and investors lost millions.
Seeing the need for a rubber that would be resistant to heat and
cold, an inventor began experimenting. But every attempt failed.

Several friends and family members lectured him about his failed
attempts and advised him that rubber was dead.

He continued to try and to fail. But years later, he accidentally
dropped a piece of rubber on a hot stove that had been treated with
sulfur. When he examined the rubber, he discovered that this
"accident" had made the rubber more resistant to cold and heat.

Through persistence and determination, Charles Goodyear created
a rubber that would be used to make Goodyear tires. He saw a need
and, despite failure, he did not give up.

There are no limits to caring ®

September 4

Jesus asked, "Weren't ten men healed? Where are the other nine? Why was this foreigner the only one who came back to thank God?" (Luke 17:17-18, CEV).

Thank You

S ome of the simplest words are very important.

How about the words, "Thank you"? Everyone likes to hear an expression of gratitude. When Mom does the laundry, does she hear, "Thanks, Mom, you're the best!" Or the teenager who cuts the lawn, works hard in school, and does things to please his parents: does he hear "thank you"?

"Thank you" is a gesture of your appreciation. How often do you express appreciation to your wife or husband? Try offering a heavy dose of "thank you" to the significant people in your life. Or how about "thank you" to the waitress or people you don't know. You'll be glad you did.

"Thank you" is one of the things we learned to say before we went to kindergarten and sometimes forget after graduating from kindergarten. Such kindness and thoughtfulness makes our community a better place to live.

There are no limits to caring ®

September 5

Today I have given you the choice between life and death, between blessings and curses.... Oh, that you would choose life, so that you and your descendants might live! (Deuteronomy 30:19, NLT).

Choices

George Jones, the late country singer, sang a great truth: "I've had choices, since the day I was born. There were voices, that taught me right from wrong. If I had listened, I wouldn't be here today, living and dying by the choices I've made!"

He's right, of course. When you consider the hereditary and environmental influences, plus all of the baggage we come here with and acquire along the way, the heaviest factor of all resides in our capacity to choose. We may be influenced by our genetic code and our surroundings, but the bottom line is – we make our choices.

Today is a good day to make choices based on our best knowledge, based on that which elevates, encourages, and affirms the best in ourselves and others. If we are going to be "living and dying by the choices we've made," then make good choices!

There are no limits to caring ®

September 6

Whoever walks with the wise becomes wise, but the companion of fools will suffer harm (Proverbs 13:20, ESV).

Jack the Parrot

Jack is a bird, a parrot that lives in Liverpool, England. One afternoon, Jerry, his owner stepped outside for some fresh air.

Jack saw the open sky and spread his wings, flying away and leaving his home behind.

Jerry searched frantically for his beloved feathered friend. It was winter and the weather was harsh and bitterly cold. He was terribly worried for Jack's safety.

Several weeks later Jerry got a call from a zoo fifteen miles away. The zookeeper had found Jack, clucking like a chicken and spending the freezing winter in the zoo's chicken coop. Parrots mimic the sounds they hear and Jack had convinced himself that he was a chicken.

Be careful of the company you keep. Don't let others bring you down. Don't be a chicken scratching in the dirt when you can soar. Each of us has wings to soar to great heights and accomplish wonderful things. Be all you can be.

September 7

A word fitly spoken is like apples of gold in a setting of silver
(Proverbs 25:11, ESV).

The Encourager

A young man with an intellectual disability, who some would not expect to accomplish much, managed to get a job, bagging groceries.

In addition to grocery bagging, this young man had a desire to encourage people. Every day, he would write out a long sheet of inspirational phrases, ideas, and thoughts. He would cut them into strips, take them to work, and place them in customers' grocery bags.

Soon, long lines formed at his register. Many wanted to be waited on by him because of the inspirational notes. Business prospered.

One person wanting to be an encourager can have a profound impact on others. People with disabilities also have certain abilities. Give a person with a disability an opportunity to demonstrate what they can do. You may find that you are the one encouraged.

September 8

There is a time for everything . . . a time to be silent and a time to speak (Ecclesiastes 3:1, 7, NIV).

Silent Treatment

A man and his wife were having some problems at home and were giving each other the silent treatment. The next week, the man realized that he would need his wife to wake him at 5:00 AM for an early flight. Not wanting to be the first to break the silence, he wrote on a piece of paper, "Please wake me at 5:00 AM."

The next morning, the man woke up, only to discover it was 9:00 AM, and that he had missed his flight. Angrily, he was about to go and see why his wife hadn't awakened him, when he noticed a piece of paper by the bed. It said, "It is 5:00 AM. Wake up!"

There is no substitute for good, forthright communication. When we don't have it, we may miss more than a flight. We could miss a great relationship. Forget the silent treatment. Today is a good day to speak in love.

There are no limits to caring ®

September 9

*The King will answer, "Whenever you did it for any of my people,
no matter how unimportant they seemed, you did it for me"*
(Matthew 25:40, CEV).

God Won't Say It

A s I was reading recently, I read this: Some things God won't ask you…

God won't ask you what kind of car you drove,
But will ask how many people you gave a lift.

God won't ask the square footage of your house,
But will ask you how many people you welcomed into your home.

God won't ask about the fancy clothes in your closet,
But will ask you how many clothes you gave to the needy.

God won't ask about your social status,
But will ask what kind of class you displayed.

God won't ask in what neighborhood you lived,
But will ask how you treated your neighbors.

God won't ask about the color of your skin,
But will ask about the content of your character.

Today, take a moment to think about how you will answer when
God speaks.

There are no limits to caring ®

September 10

Let us strip off every weight that slows us down, especially the sin
that so easily trips us up. And let us run with endurance the race
God has set before us (Hebrews 12:1, NLT).

Run

A mother looked into her back yard and saw her five children gathered in a circle, staring at the ground. She walked out to see what had captured their interest. When she got close enough, to her horror she saw they had found a litter of baby skunks. She screamed and yelled at the top of her voice, "Run children, run!" Startled by her scream, each child grabbed a baby skunk and ran!

Before we run, there are things we need to leave behind. We should leave behind those things that cause a big stink, those things that divide us, - our past mistakes, past hurts, and anger.

Some things we should never leave behind, like our children, or those people who are hurting or confused.

"Run children, run!" But we must run together, leaving some things behind and making sure we take with us the things that really matter.

There are no limits to caring ®

266

September 11

I pray that the eyes of your heart may be enlightened in order that you may know the hope to which he has called you (Ephesians 1:18, NIV).

Don't Give Up

Port Authority Police Sgt. John McLoughlin was the last person pulled alive from the collapsed World Trade Center. He was interviewed from the hospital after four months of treatment and care. He called his rescue a miracle. He was buried under 30 feet of debris, pinned from his hips to his feet in a tiny cavern "the size of his body."

During his ordeal, he said there was a time of acceptance of dying, but when he thought of his family, he knew he had to live for them.

When asked what lesson he had learned as a result of the ordeal, he said, "Don't give up. There is always hope."

The sergeant was right. Hope is what keeps us going when nothing else will and when all else fails. No matter how dark the night, no matter how impossible the circumstances, do not give up hope. It makes the difference.

There are no limits to caring ®

September 12

I know that you can do all things, and that no purpose of yours can be thwarted (Job 42:2, ESV).

Rent-A-Husband

Parade magazine recently carried the story of Cale Warren, Jr., who started the very successful home repair business called, "Rent-A-Husband."

Warren was once the owner of a thriving construction business. A serious auto accident prevented him from working. And he lost everything: his business, his home, and even his marriage. He was homeless, sleeping in a vacant warehouse, working odd jobs, just to get by.

One night, he got the idea for a home repair business: *RENT-A-HUSBAND, FOR THOSE JOBS THAT NEVER GET DONE.* Starting from scratch in 1996, he built his business into a national, home-repair franchise.

Warren says, "My story says, 'never give up hope because you are never out of the game.' I don't care how far down you get; your life can turn around in a heartbeat—as long as you don't give up on yourself."

Good advice. Don't give up on yourself. Today is another day of opportunity

There are no limits to caring ®

September 13

This means that anyone who belongs to Christ has become a new person. The old life is gone; a new life has begun! (2 Corinthians 5:17, NLT)

James Carter

James Carter left his rural Louisiana home at the age of 13. He found himself on hard times, and in 1959, was serving time in the Mississippi State Penitentiary.

Working on the chain gang, Carter would often sing to help pass the time and make the work more bearable. On one such occasion, a musicologist made a recording of Carter leading the work gang in the song, "Po Lazarus."

Decades later, that recording was incorporated into the movie soundtrack of "O Brother, Where Art Thou?" Carter, in the meantime, had straightened out his life, retired as a shipping clerk, and lived quietly with his minister wife and three daughters.

In 2002, James received a Platinum Disc and his first royalty check for $20,000, and when the soundtrack won 6 Grammy's, Carter's name was on one of them.

A man's past does not have to seal his fate. Good things can evolve out of bad circumstances.

There are no limits to caring ®

September 14

Blessed is the nation whose God is the LORD (Psalm 33:12, ESV).

Star-Spangled Banner

During the War of 1812, the British fleet lay off the shores of Baltimore, intent on attacking Fort McHenry. The American commander of the fort had ordered a huge American flag, so it could be easily seen by the British. The flag, with its 15 stars, measured 30X42 feet.

The attack began on September 13, 1814, as Francis Scott Key watched the battle from eight miles away. When the shelling ceased at dawn, he feared the fort had fallen. Raising his telescope just in time to see the wind catch the huge flag, he knew that the fort was secure.

Francis Scott Key was so inspired that he wrote the words that became our national anthem. That song, and the sight of our flag, have brought great inspiration to us in recent days. The Star-Spangled Banner still waves o'er the land of the free, and the home of the brave.

There are no limits to caring ®

September 15

But I say to you who hear, Love your enemies, do good to those who hate you (Luke 6:27, ESV).

How to Wash the Cat

Guess who wrote:

HOW TO WASH THE CAT?

1. Thoroughly clean the toilet.
2. Lift both lids and add shampoo.
3. Find and soothe cat as you carry him to the bathroom.
4. In one swift move, place cat in toilet, close both lids and stand on top so cat cannot escape.
5. The cat will self-agitate and produce ample suds. (Ignore ruckus from inside toilet; cat is having fun).
6. Flush 3 or 4 times, this provides power rinse which is quite effective.
7. Have someone open the outside door, stand as far from toilet as possible, and quickly lift both lids.
8. Clean cat will rocket out of the toilet and outdoors, where he will air dry.

Signed…The Dog

Take it from the cat, not everyone is your friend. Stay close to the people who love you. They won't flush you down the drain.

There are no limits to caring ®

September 16

Truthful words stand the test of time, but lies are soon exposed
(Proverbs 12:18, NLT).

Weather Report

Guess who wrote:

HOW TO GET A CURRENT WEATHER REPORT

You want a current weather report?
- Go to your back door and look for the dog. If the dog is at the door and he is wet, it's probably raining.
- But if the dog is standing there really soaking wet, it is probably raining really hard.
- If the dog's fur looks like it is rubbed the wrong way, it's probably windy.
- If the dog has snow on his back, it's probably snowing.

Of course, to be able to tell the weather like this, you must leave the dog outside *all the time…especially if you expect bad weather.* So, who wrote this?

THE CAT.

Take it from the dog, or the cat, not everyone has your best interest at heart. Hang tight with those you know love you. They won't shut you out in the cold… or rain!

There are no limits to caring ®

September 17

The wolf shall dwell with the lamb, and the leopard shall lie down with the young goat, and the calf and the lion and the fattened calf together (Isaiah 11:6, ESV).

Dogs and Cats

Wouldn't it be wonderful if we lived in a world where there was mutual trust, where the dog and cat were best of buds?

Wouldn't it be wonderful if we didn't have to worry about being flushed down the drain or left in the cold?

Wouldn't it be wonderful if we could trust our investment in big corporations? Our economy depends on trusting what people say. Sometimes, there is a fear that the books have been cooked—inflated.

Counting on what people say starts with each of us telling the truth. We must tell the truth and teach our kids to tell the truth. That's an old-fashioned value that could save us billions of dollars.

When we tell the truth, the lamb can lay down with the lion, and the dog and cat can be best of friends.

There are no limits to caring ®

September 18

Gracious words are a honeycomb, sweet to the soul and healing to the bones (Proverbs 16:24, NIV).

What Really Matters

A wife finally convinced her husband to let her take his shiny little red sports car out for a spin. He agreed, but she was nervous because that little car was his pride and joy.

Sure enough, she had a fender bender. She was distraught. It was all her fault, and she dreaded confronting her husband. She reached into the glove compartment to retrieve the insurance and registration papers. On top of the papers was a note in her husband's handwriting. It was addressed to her and said, "Honey, if you are reading this, you have probably had an accident. I hope and pray you are OK. Remember, it's you I love, not the car!"

Those words came from a man who understood what really matters. Never forget what counts. Things can be replaced. People cannot. Relationships are more important than things.

There are no limits to caring ®

September 19

Delight yourself in the LORD, and he will give you the desires of your heart.
(Psalms 37:4, ESV).

James Irwin

One evening after dinner, young James was playing in the living room as his parents were cleaning up the kitchen.

His mother, glancing at the clock, asked him to go up to bed, telling him that she'd check in on him later.

James went straight upstairs to his room to get ready for bed. An hour or so later, his mother came up to check on him, and, to her astonishment, found that he was staring quietly out of his window at the moon.

"What are you doing, James?" she asked. "I'm looking at the moon, Mommy, and one day I'm going to walk on the moon."

Thirty-two years later, James Irwin walked on the moon. He is one of 12 people who walked on the moon. Follow your dreams. Work hard. Strive to achieve what you've always imagined. Shoot for the moon and one day you may just do it.

There are no limits to caring ®

September 20

Bear with one another and forgive one another if any of you has a grievance against someone. Forgive as the Lord forgave you (Colossians 3:13, NIV).

Fences or Bridges

Two brothers worked adjoining farms in harmony for many years. Then a small misunderstanding became a major family feud. The younger brother, in an effort to stop the madness, diverted a creek into a meadow between the two farms, creating a permanent barrier between them.

One morning, a carpenter came to the older brother and asked for work. The older brother said, "Well, my brother diverted that creek to separate our farms, so I'll go him one better. Let's build a high fence."

"I think I understand the situation," said the carpenter, as he began work.

When the older brother returned that evening, he found a bridge over the creek! As he walked toward the bridge, instead of the high fence he had asked for, he saw his estranged brother coming across the bridge, holding out his arms saying, "Thank you for building the bridge to bring us together."

Building fences or bridges—that's the choice we make daily.

There are no limits to caring ®

September 21

I thank my God every time I remember you (Philippians 1:3, NIV).

What Matters Most

Here's a quiz: 1) Name the world's wealthiest person. 2) Name the last Heisman trophy winner. 3) Name the last Miss America. 4) Name the last person to win the Nobel Prize. 5) Name the last Academy Award winners for best actor and actress.

So, how did you do? The point is, none of us remember the headlines of yesterday. Applause dies. Awards tarnish. Achievements are forgotten.

Here's the real quiz: 1) Name a teacher who aided your journey through school. 2) Name two friends who helped you through a tough time. 3) Name two people who have made you feel appreciated. 4) Name three people who taught you something worthwhile.

Easier? Sure! The lesson: The people you remember are the ones that care for you. The way you will be remembered is the way you cared for others.

There are no limits to caring ®

September 22

If you forgive others for the wrongs they do to you, your Father in heaven will forgive you (Matthew 6:14, CEV).

Heavy Bag

A teacher had each student bring a clear plastic bag and a sack of potatoes. He said, "For every person you have refused to forgive in your life, write their name on a potato and put it in the plastic bag." Some of the bags were quite heavy.

He told the students to take the bags everywhere they went. Even to bed at night. The hassle of lugging the potato bag around was a constant reminder of the burden of an unforgiving heart. Eventually the potatoes deteriorated into a slimy mess.

This is a great picture of the price we pay for an unforgiving heart. Often, we think of forgiveness as something we give to another. Actually, it's a gift to ourselves more than anyone else.

The next time you think you can't forgive someone, ask yourself, "Isn't my bag already heavy enough?"

There are no limits to caring ®

September 23

Happy are the people whose God is the Lord! (Psalm 144:15, NKJV).

───────※※※───────

Choose Happiness

A 92-year-old lady moved into a nursing home after her husband passed away. She was legally blind, but always managed to look her best with great class.

When Mrs. Jones was ushered into her new room by staff, she said, "I just love it!" But "Mrs. Jones, you can't see the room, how do you know you love it?" Mrs. Jones replied, "Seeing it has nothing to do with it. Whether I love my room doesn't depend on the furniture or how it is arranged…it's how I arrange my mind. I've already decided to love it and be happy. Happiness is something you choose ahead of time."

Today, each of us can choose how we will arrange our minds. Why not choose to arrange your mind with happiness? Just choose happiness—it's a mind thing. You will be blessed, and so will your family and friends.

There are no limits to caring ®

September 24

Pride goes before destruction, and a haughty spirit before a fall
(Proverbs 16:18, ESV).

Frog in the Mouth

In a certain pond lived two wild ducks and a frog, the best of friends.

When the hot summer came, the pond began to dry up. They realized that they would have to move. The ducks could easily fly to another pond, but what about their friend, the frog?

Finally, it was decided that the ducks would put the two ends of a stick in their bills. Then the frog could hang onto the middle of the stick with his mouth, and the ducks would fly him to another pond.

As they were flying low, a farmer looked up; and when he saw the strange formation, he said, "Well, isn't that a clever idea! I wonder who thought of that?" The frog opened his big mouth and said, "I did!"

The Bible warns us, "Pride goes before a fall." Humility carries us a long way.

There are no limits to caring ®

September 25

How beautiful on the mountains are the feet of the messenger who brings good news, the good news of peace and salvation, the news that the God of Israel reigns! (Isaiah 52:7, NLT).

Carrier

West Nile Virus is commonly spread by mosquitoes who carry this virus. That's scary.

However, some contagious things are wonderful.

- A smile is contagious. Just carry a smile. And the world smiles too.
- How about being a carrier of encouragement? We could use an epidemic of encouragement.
- How about being a carrier of peace and good will? We could certainly use an outbreak of peace and goodwill.
- How about being a carrier of integrity! Don't you think our current political scene could use an epidemic of integrity?
- And wouldn't it be wonderful if we could be responsible for infecting others with love and compassion?

These infections make people and communities well, not sick. Today you can be a carrier of a smile, encouragement, integrity, peace and good will, love and compassion.

September 26

If you have faith like a grain of mustard seed, you will say to this mountain, "Move for here to there," and it will move, and nothing will be impossible for you (Matthew 17:20, ESV).

Motivation

There's a great old story about a man who got off work at midnight and walked home through the cemetery each night. One night, he did not realize that, during the day, a grave had been dug in the very center of his path.

Sure enough, he fell in. Try as he might, he could not climb out. Soon he became tired and decided to relax until morning. The town drunk happened to travel the same path and also fell in. The drunk began frantically trying to claw his way out. The other man reached out, touched the drunk and said, "You can't get out of here."

But he did! The right kind of motivation will work miracles. Sometimes the motivation is fear. At other times, it's a word of encouragement.

For me, it's seeing someone helping someone else. Makes me want to do the same thing. What motivates you to be your best?

There are no limits to caring ®

September 27

*There is nothing hidden that will not be made public. There is no
secret that will not be well known* (Mark 4:22, CEV).

Skinny Dipping

An old farmer had owned a farm for many years. He had a large
lake in the back forty, and the lake was a great place to swim.
One evening, the farmer decided to go down to the lake. As he
neared the lake, he heard shouting and laughing. As he came
closer, he saw it was a group of young women, skinny-dipping.

He made the women aware of his presence. They all immediately
swam to the deep end of the lake. One of the women shouted,
"We're not coming out until you leave."

The old man replied, "I didn't come down here to watch you ladies
swim or make you get out of the lake, I only came to feed the
alligators."

Communication is important—and effective communication often
leads to a change in plans—particularly when we get the whole
story.

There are no limits to caring ®

September 28

For you know that the testing of your faith produces steadfastness
(James 1:3, ESV).

The Reef

The Great Barrier Reef stretches some 1,800 miles from New Guinea to Australia. One visitor to the reef asked the tour guide, "Why does the water on one side of the reef look pale and lifeless, and the water on the ocean side look vibrant and strong?

The guide answered, "The coral around the lagoon is in still water, with no challenge for its survival. It dies early. The coral on the ocean side is constantly being tested by wind and waves. It has to fight for survival every day. It has to change and adapt. As a result, it grows healthy and strong. It reproduces. That's the way it is with every living organism."

The guide was right. Challenged and tested, we come alive! Like coral pounded by the sea, we grow. If you are going through tough times in your life, be encouraged and know that you can be stronger for that experience.

There are no limits to caring ®

September 29

*For wisdom is better than jewels, and all that you may desire
cannot compare with her* (Proverbs 8:11, ESV).

Noah's Ark

R emember Noah's Ark? We can learn everything we need to
know about life from Noah's Ark. Here's what we can learn:

- Don't miss the boat.
- Remember that we are all in the same boat.
- Plan ahead. It wasn't raining when Noah built the ark.
- Stay fit. When you're 600 years old, someone may ask you
  to do something really big.
- Don't listen to critics; just get on with the job.
- Build your future on high ground.
- For safety sake, travel in pairs.
- Speed isn't always an advantage. The snails were on board
  with the cheetahs.
- When you are stressed, float awhile.
- Remember, the Ark was built by amateurs, the Titanic by
  professionals.
- No matter the storm, when you are with God, there's always
  a rainbow waiting.

Great lessons. They will "float your boat" when you find yourself
in life's deepest water.

There are no limits to caring ®

September 30

Agree wholeheartedly with each other, loving one another, and working together with one mind and purpose (Philippians 2:2, NLT).

Keep Marriage Alive

At a recent seminar that I conducted, a participant raised the question, "How can my wife and I keep our marriage alive and well and not experience divorce years from now?" My response was, "Your spouse must be the most important person in your life, and there must be an unrealistic belief that she is the greatest."

I said unrealistic belief – why not? We have so many other things that are not rational – why not believe your spouse is the best? She just may be. Of course, that response was addressed to a somewhat healthy relationship, free from abuse. I think this concept applies to far more people than not. Try making your spouse number one and believe in him or her – as the best.

You know, I have known folks like that. They always seem to be the happiest people.

October 1

There is neither Jew nor Greek, there is neither slave nor free,
there is no male and female, for you are all one in Christ Jesus
(Galatians 3:28, ESV).

Parachute

Charles Plumb was a Navy Pilot shot down over Vietnam. He parachuted into enemy hands and spent 6 years as a prisoner of war. He survived and now lectures on lessons learned from that experience.

One day a man came to him and said, "I am the guy who packed your last parachute. I guess it worked!" Plumb assured him that it did and thanked him. He couldn't sleep that night for thinking about the man who packed his parachute. As an officer, he had no doubt passed that sailor on board the ship many times, but never spoke to him or even knew what his job was.

Today, Plumb poses the question to his audiences, "Who's packing your parachute?" Great question! Who are those who pack our parachutes, our life support system?

Parents, family, teachers, colleagues. Have you thanked them? Today find those support people in your life and thank them.

There are no limits to caring ®

October 2

I press on toward the goal to win the prize of God's heavenly calling in Christ Jesus (Philippians 3:14, ESV).

Keep Trying

Six-year-old Brandon decided one Saturday morning to fix breakfast for his parents. He wanted to make pancakes. He got out the flour, but spilled it. He got the eggs, but dropped them. He got the milk, and sure enough, managed to spill it too. He had managed to make a horrible, white, sticky mess. He had gotten it all over the floor and himself.

When he looked up and saw his dad standing in the door, he began to cry. He was afraid he was going to be scolded and maybe even spanked. But his dad just walked over, picked him up, and thanked him for what he intended to do. Because of his dad's response, Brandon will probably try to make pancakes again.

Just because we mess up, we can't stop trying to "make pancakes." Sooner or later we'll get it right, and then we will be glad we tried.

There are no limits to caring ®

October 3

Therefore, just as through one man sin entered into the world, and death through sin, and so death spread to all men, because all sinned (Romans 5:12, NASB).

Mouse Trap

A mouse saw a farmer and his wife setting a mousetrap. He ran into the barnyard shouting, "There's a mouse trap in the house!"

The chicken clucked, "It's of no consequence to me." The pig was sympathetic, but said, "All I can do is pray about it." The cow said, "Sounds like YOUR problem, not mine."

Later that night, the mousetrap snapped. The farmer's wife ran in to find a venomous snake caught by its tail. The snake bit her. She grew deathly ill.

The farmer killed the chicken to make soup to nurse her back to health. Neighbors came to sit with her, so he butchered the pig in order to feed them. When his wife died, he slaughtered the cow to feed those who came to the funeral.

Just remember that when the least of us is threatened, we are all at risk.

There are no limits to caring ®

October 4

With their mouths the godless destroy their neighbors, but through knowledge the righteous escape (Proverbs 11:9, NIV).

Church Gossip

Sarah, the church gossip and self-appointed supervisor of the church's morals, kept sticking her nose into other people's business. However, the old members feared her enough to maintain their silence.

But, she made a mistake when she accused a new member, George, of being an alcoholic after she saw his pickup truck parked in front of a bar one afternoon. She commented to George, and others, that everyone seeing it there would know that he was an alcoholic. George, a man of few words, stared at her for a moment and just walked away. He said nothing.

Later that evening, George quietly parked his pickup in front of Sarah's house...and left it there all night.

Before we condemn, maybe we should walk in another person's shoes. Sometimes, things are not the way they seem. But even drunks and prostitutes need love and compassion, not condemnation.

There are no limits to caring ®

October 5

You obey the law of Christ when you offer each other a helping hand (Galatians 6:2, CEV).

Gene and Elmer

Two grumpy old men weren't really grumpy, just old. Gene found peace after a battle with cancer. When he was diagnosed with cancer, his friend Elmer moved Gene into his home to care for him. And in the later days, Elmer slept on the floor right by Gene—taking care of him through the night. Even to the end, Gene had whatever he needed—because his buddy made sure that he went lacking for nothing.

One couldn't read or write, one was highly educated.
One was poor, one was rich.
One had a faith early in life, one found faith late in life (because of his friend).
One was black, one was white.
They were a model of who we all must be—despite profound differences.

My dad, Elmer, was a model for his son.

He taught me…there are no limits to caring—even for people who are different.

There are no limits to caring ®

October 6

If you believe, you will receive whatever you ask for in prayer.
(Matthew 21:22, NIV).

A Miracle

A father, from a poor family, summoned his daughter Tess. He told her that her brother was very sick. The brother had something growing in his head, and it would take a miracle to save him.

Tess took her piggy bank containing $1.11 to the local pharmacy and told the druggist that her brother was sick, and she wanted to buy a miracle. The druggist told her he was sorry, but he didn't sell miracles.

However, the brother of the druggist was standing there and asked the little girl how much money she had. She told him $1.11. He said, "Why that's the exact cost of a miracle for little brothers."

This man was Dr. Carlton Armstrong, a neurosurgeon.

He operated without charge, and the younger brother made a full recovery. The mother said, "That surgery was a real miracle. I wonder how much it would have cost."

Tess knew…$1.11, plus a child's faith.

October 7

But let all who take refuge in you rejoice; let them ever sing for joy, and spread your protection over them (Psalm 5:11, ESV).

Surviving

Linda Ellerbee, a noted journalist, offered six ways to survive in a changing world. Keep in mind that her philosophy was formed while raising children as a single mom, pioneering in the man's world of television journalism, and surviving breast cancer.

She said:

1. If you believe you are right, fight all the way! You may be right.
2. Realize the best things in life are not THINGS! Treat people with respect.
3. It is the duty of every citizen to keep your mouth open!
4. If you want to grow old, don't mellow.
5. If you know what you stand for, and are willing to stand firm, you can win.
6. In this world, a good time to laugh is any time you can!

Good advice. Seems like she has done more than just "survive."

There are no limits to caring ®

October 8

If we confess our sins, he is faithful and just to forgive our sins and to cleanse us from all unrighteousness (1 John 1:9, ESV).

Stolen Rope

A man weighted down with the guilt of his own mistakes went to confess his sins to the Priest. "Father, I have stolen a rope." However, he neglected to confess that there was a cow at the other end of the rope!

Perhaps it is most difficult to be honest with ourselves. When we spin the truth, we fool ourselves. We have an unusual capacity for self-deception.

How about the person who says:

- "I only had a beer or two before the wreck—I was in complete control."
- Or the abusive husband who said, "She had it coming."
- Or the person who threw trash on the road, saying, "Well, I pay taxes."
- Or the man who voted against a tax increase because "We have waste and abuse." And yet, Alabama pays less tax than any other state.

The stolen rope is only the beginning. The truth always sets us free.

There are no limits to caring ®

October 9

*And after you have suffered a little while, the God of all grace,
who has called you to his eternal glory in Christ, will himself
restore, confirm, strengthen, and establish you* (1 Peter 5:10,
ESV).

Weathered

A man approached a farmer about buying his dilapidated old barn. The farmer wanted to know what he wanted with such an old barn. The years of exposure to the elements had taken its toll. After all, the paint had long vanished, and the wood had turned silver gray.

The man replied, "That's exactly why I want it. You can't get paint to produce that color. Only years of exposure to sun, wind and rain can produce wood that beautiful. I want to panel the den of my new home with that old wood."

So it is with our lives. We complain about aging and the trials and tribulations that we have to face. Yet, those challenges are the very things that produce strength and character in us.

As we face the struggles and trials of life, our faith in God can produce the beauty of character that only comes by weathering the storms of life.

There are no limits to caring ®

October 10

You will seek me and find me when you seek me with all your heart (Jeremiah 19:13, NIV).

Missing God

Joey, a young 8-year-old boy, had been getting into a lot of trouble. In desperation, the mother decided that she would send him to see her pastor. And so, the mother got an appointment for her young son to see the pastor, having told the pastor the problem.

As the young lad sat in the pastor's office, with a solemn deep voice, the pastor said, "Where is God?" And Joey just sat there. And three times, the pastor asked, "Where is God?" On the third time, Joey bolted and ran.

He ran home, upstairs, and hid in the closet. His older brother, Benny, came in and found him in the closet and said, "What are you doing?" Joey said, "We are in big trouble…I mean, real big trouble this time!" "What happened?" asked Benny. "God is missing, and they think we had something to do with it!"

Is God missing in your life? Invite him in! It's your choice.

There are no limits to caring ®

October 11

*He was a Levite from Cyprus, and the apostles called him
Barnabas, which means "one who encourages others"* (Acts
4:36, CEV).

Not Perfect

Carl's dad was 94 when he died. He had been a good man and
a great dad. At the funeral, Carl saw many friends from the
past, including his former school principal, who was now 76 years
old.

He reminded his former principal, "More than 45 years ago, you
gave me my first and only paddling in school." The old educator
replied, "Well, I might have been out of line." "No sir, I learned
my lesson and was never in trouble again."

A great story. A principal said, "I could have made a mistake."
That's big. A student replied, "No you didn't; what you did made
a positive difference in my life." That's big.

 Carl's dad had a profound impact on his son's life, but so did a
principal, who didn't see himself as perfect.

October 12

By this we know love, that he laid down his life for us, and we ought to lay down our lives for the brothers (1 John 3:16, ESV).

Caring and Tough Love

There are no limits to caring. Each day, that's the message. There are no limits to caring. But how is it lived out in the everyday world?

For the spouse who is abused, it may mean that he/she begins to care for self—and moves out of a destructive relationship. That may be the first step to finding no limits to caring.

For the family of the alcoholic, it may mean to let that person hit bottom—without a parachute. Only at the bottom can one begin to find the way up.

For the adult kid who won't grow up—who won't leave home—it may mean letting that person experience the challenges of life without a rescue attempt. It's called tough love.

The only problem with tough love is that it is equally tough on the person who gives. Tough love is tough for those who demonstrate there are no limits to caring.

There are no limits to caring ®

October 13

Be kind to one another, tenderhearted, forgiving one another, as
God in Christ forgave you (Ephesians 4:32, ESV).

Gloria-Robber

Gloria was a good and caring person. She always tried to be kind to people. One day, she was at the mall shopping – one of her favorite pastimes. In the parking lot as she was leaving, a man came up to her, put a gun in her face and said, "Give me your money!"

Now, it's never a good time to rob someone, but especially when they're leaving the mall! So, Gloria said, "Sir, I only have two dollars, but I'll be glad to write you a check." The would-be robber became so frustrated, he ran away.

Just goes to show, it pays to be kind, even to enemies. There would probably be fewer enemies if there was more kindness. Kindness is something that we all want. It changes who we are, and it changes those around us. "Be kind to one another, tenderhearted."

There are no limits to caring ®

October 14

If you help the poor, you are lending to the LORD--and he will repay you! (Proverbs 19:17, NLT).

Something for Others

I stopped at a local sandwich shop for lunch. As I sat there, a man and his son entered and asked the manager for some free food. The manager replied he had no food to give. I thought, "I need to buy this man and his son some food." I informed the manager I would pay for whatever they wanted. They ate, thanked me, and went on their way.

As I was leaving, a man seated in the corner called me over. He said, "I caught some fresh shrimp today I want to give to you."

"Why? I don't know you." He said, "But I saw you give food to those in need, and I have a need to give to you."

"What do you mean?" I asked. He said, "You know, that's the way it works."

That *is* the way it works. When you give, you cannot help but receive. Find a way to give today.

There are no limits to caring ®

October 15

Whatever happens, keep thanking God because of Jesus Christ.
This is what God wants you to do (1 Thessalonians 5:18, CEV).

Other Doors

A family felt blessed, even though they had a young child with serious medical problems. As stressful as their trips were to the hospital – they felt grateful. Why? Because some doors, they didn't have to go through.

They didn't go through:

- Doors where children were treated for serious burns.
- Doors that lead to children who spend their childhoods battling cancer.
- Doors that lead to children in ICU.

Every day, people would walk through those doors, but this family was able to keep walking past those doors. The family was thankful, because there were hundreds of other doors that were far worse than the door they passed through. And they could have been passing through any one of those other doors. Pray for strength to pass through the doors you face, but be sure to thank God for the doors you don't pass through.

There are no limits to caring ®

October 16

Don't put it off; do it now! Don't rest until you do (Proverbs 6:4, NLT).

Make It Happen

In the airport, Jack witnessed a man greeting his family. One by one, he embraced each of his three children and told them how much he loved them and had missed them. He then gave his wife a long, passionate kiss. Jack, seeing this wonderful display of love and affection, asked the man, "How long have you been married, and how long have you been away?" "We've been married twelve years, and I have been away two whole days!"

Two days? Jack was stunned and said, "I hope my marriage is still that passionate after twelve years!" The man suddenly stopped, looked Jack straight in the eye, and with forcefulness, said, "Don't hope; make it happen."

Many times, we say "we hope," or "we wish," but we don't make it happen. Today is the time for you to make it happen for your family.

There are no limits to caring ®

October 17

A fool's mouth is his ruin, and his lips are a snare to his soul
(Proverbs 18:7, ESV).

Pastor's Mother

An elderly lady walked into the local country church. The
friendly usher greeted her at the door and helped her up the
flight of steps.

"Where would you like to sit?" he asked politely.
"The front row please." she answered.
"You really don't want to do that," the usher said. "The pastor is
really boring."
"Do you happen to know who I am?" the woman inquired.
"No," he said.
"I'm the pastor's mother," she replied.
"Do you know who I am?" he asked.
"No," she said.
"Good," he responded.

You never know who might be listening to you—it could be
someone's mama.

Words can be either hurtful or uplifting. Remember Mama's
words, "If you don't have something nice to say, don't say
anything at all." It is always better to say something positive
about a person, then you don't have to worry about who might
hear you.

There are no limits to caring ®

October 18

Spouting off before listening to the facts is both shameful and
foolish
(Proverbs 18:13, NLT).

A Brick

A young executive was driving through a neighborhood in his new Jaguar. He watched for kids and slowed down when he thought he saw something. As his car passed, a brick smashed into his side door.

He slammed on the brakes and spun to where the brick was thrown. He jumped out, shouting, "What are you doing?" "This is a new car and it's gonna cost you."

"I'm sorry, I didn't know what to do!" pleaded the child. "I threw it because no one would stop. My brother is in a wheelchair and rolled off the curb and fell out. He is hurt, and I can't lift him. Will you please help me?"

Moved to tears, the man helped them, but he never repaired his door. He kept the dent to remind himself not to go through life so fast that someone has to throw a brick at you to get your attention.

There are no limits to caring ®

October 19

Give to the one who begs from you, and do not refuse the one who would borrow from you (Matthew 5:42, ESV).

Don't We All

Joe was putting groceries in his car, when he saw a ragged street person approaching. Joe thought, "I hope he doesn't ask for money." The street person sat down at a nearby bus stop. He looked over at Joe's car and said, "Nice car." But the plea for money never came.

Joe looked at him and thought, "He probably doesn't have any money to ride the bus." He felt like he needed to offer him something, so Joe said, "Do you need any help?" The street person smiled and said, "Don't we all?"

So true. We all need help. Maybe not for bus fare or a place to sleep, but we all need help from time to time. And equally true, we need to offer help. Maybe a few dollars to someone in need, or just a word of encouragement. It has to do with caring. And, there are no limits to caring.

There are no limits to caring ®

October 20

These are evil times, so make every minute count (Ephesians 5:16, CEV).

Missed Opportunities

A young man wished to marry a farmer's daughter. The farmer said, "Go stand in that field, and I will release three bulls. If you catch one of them by the tail, you can marry my daughter."

The young man stood and waited. The gate opened, and the first bull was so big and mean looking, he decided to let him pass. The gate opened again, and the second bull looked meaner than the first. He let him pass as well. The third bull came out, and the young man smiled. It was the scrawniest bull he had ever seen. When the bull came by, he grabbed for its tail...but it had no tail!

Life is full of opportunities. Some will be more challenging than others. But once we let them pass in hopes of finding something easier, we may miss them altogether.

October 21

Jesus said, "They need not go away; you give them something to eat." They said to him, "We have only five loaves here and two fish" (Matthew 14:16-17, ESV).

Osceola

Osceola McCarty was a grammar school dropout, but she managed to save $150,000 by doing laundry and ironing. She gave all of her savings to create a scholarship fund at the University of Southern Mississippi. She said, "I can't do everything, but I can do something to help somebody. And what I can do, I will do."

When the story of her gift made the news, more than six hundred other donors added over $330,000 to the original scholarship fund. Ted Turner, the founder of CNN, was inspired to donate a billion dollars to the UN Health and Population programs. He said, "If that little woman can give away everything she has, then I can give a billion!"

Osceola McCarty's gift was inspiring and infectious. She demonstrated there are no limits to caring. Just imagine what YOUR gift might do!

There are no limits to caring ®

October 22

The godly may trip seven times, but they will get up again
(Proverbs 24:16, NLT).

Vaughn

October 22, 2005 was not John Vaughn's best night. He was the kicker for the Auburn football team. That night, Auburn played LSU. Vaughn missed five field goals! The last one gave LSU the victory.

Swirling winds played a factor. But Vaughn didn't make excuses. He said, "I've got to work harder."

The next day, after church, Coach Tuberville noticed Vaughn on the field. At each place where he had missed a field goal, he practiced 10 kicks. He wanted to get it right.

A few weeks later, in the game against Georgia, he kicked the winning field goal. Auburn won by one point, one kick, one player who knew how to handle his mistakes.

How do you handle your mistakes?
Blame it on the swirling wind?
Run from your mistakes?
Feel sorry for yourself?
Pretend like it didn't happen?
Blame the dog, the kids or the wife?

When we take responsibility for our mistakes and change our behavior, then we can win the big games.

There are no limits to caring ®

October 23

I will give you the keys of the kingdom of heaven (Matthew 16:19, ESV).

A Key

Some friends recently joined a small church in North Alabama. When they were presented to the church as new members, the pastor handed them a key to the church and said, "You are now family, and here is your key to the house!" Wow! How many churches would, or could do that?

That church is making an important statement about acceptance, equality and trust. Those ingredients must be present in every family. After all, acceptance, equality and trust make a group of people a family.

Unfortunately, that openness and acceptance may not be found in many churches, nor in a lot of families. However, it can be. You hold the key; it is your attitude. Today, you can give your neighbors, your children, or your parents the permission to enter your life. Use your "attitude key" to let people in, don't lock them out. Give them a key.

There are no limits to caring ®

October 24

And I told them of the hand of my God that had been upon me for good.... And they said, "Let us rise up and build." So they strengthened their hands for the good work (Nehemiah 2:18, ESV).

Bridges

On my way to work, I have the privilege of watching a bridge being built, creating a new road. I am fascinated by the bridge building. It takes a lot of time, a lot of energy, planning, and hard work. Bridge building is not something that is done overnight, or in ignorance.

But each of us needs to be about building bridges every day. Building bridges
- to those who are less fortunate
- to those whom we have alienated
- to those who have done us wrong
- to those whom we work with
- to those whom we live with

The truth is anyone can make a mess, but few have learned the art of building bridges.

Burning bridges behind us doesn't get it. We may need to get out of town on one of those bridges.

Our challenge is to build bridges, not burn bridges. You will be a better person for every bridge you build today.

There are no limits to caring ®

October 25

Then, because so many people were coming and going that they did not even have a chance to eat, he said to them, "Come with me by yourselves to a quiet place and get some rest." (Mark 6:31, NIV).

Sharp Axe

Two men were hired to cut down trees. The contract called for them to be paid per tree. Bill grunted and sweated and swung his axe relentlessly. Ed, on the other hand, seemed to be working about half as fast. Every so often, he took a rest and sat down for a few minutes.

At the end of the day, Bill was terribly sore, but Ed was smiling and telling jokes. And amazingly, Ed had cut down more trees! Bill said, "I noticed you sitting, while I worked without a break. How did you outwork me?" Ed smiled and said, "Did you notice that while I was sitting, I was sharpening my axe?"

In order to reach our greatest potential, we have to stop along the way, for rest, recreation—or to be re-created and renewed. Only when we take time to sharpen our axe can we be at our best.

There are no limits to caring ®

October 26

John told them, "If you have two coats, give one to someone who doesn't have any. If you have food, share it with someone else"
(Luke 3:11, CEV).

Make a Difference Day

October 26 is National Make a Difference Day. The day is designed to meet needs and make a difference in someone's life. There are many things you and I can do to make a difference in someone's life.

- Take a widow, shut in, single parent, or adult to lunch
- Baby-sit for a young couple
- Put a thank you note in your mailbox for your postman
- Pay for another person's meal
- Help someone with something they are unable to do on their own
- Compliment someone on their accomplishments, their looks, or their smile
- Send a card to a shut-in
- Send a letter of appreciation to someone who has made a difference in your life

There are always opportunities to make a positive difference in someone's life. It's a way to demonstrate, there are no limits to caring.

There are no limits to caring ®

October 27

And the LORD blessed the latter days of Job more than his beginning.
(Job 42:12, ESV).

Paul Hamm

Paul Hamm spent his life getting ready for the Olympics. But in Athens he lost it all. With one stumble on a vault that he had never botched before, Hamm lost it all. He dropped from 1st place to 12th place. No possible way to win a metal.

How did he feel? "I was very upset and depressed," he said. "I felt like I let myself down."

What did he do? He didn't let his feelings control his behavior. He didn't give up. He turned the impossible to possible. He came back with the best performance of his life and won the gold.

There are times in our lives when we feel hopeless and defeated, like we have let ourselves down. But it doesn't have to be over. Using discipline, skills and determination, you can achieve your best after a defeat. Don't give up. Give your best.

There are no limits to caring ®

October 28

But whoever listens to me will dwell secure and will be at ease,
without dread of disaster (Proverbs 1:33, ESV).

Traffic Jam

Several years ago, my wife and I headed north on I-65. We encountered two major wrecks on the interstate, less than 2 miles apart. Forty-five minutes later we made it through the traffic jam, only to encounter major rainstorms.

We were delighted to get on the other side of the wrecks and storms, but we became anxious when we realized that our daughter was traveling the same route. She too must go through the same storms and the same traffic jam.

Or must she? We called her on the cell, told her what she was facing. Because she listened to us, she was able to find an alternative route—no traffic jams, no storms.

Sometimes our kids listen to what we tell them. Sometimes they don't. If we learn to listen to those who have gone before us, we can make wise and better decisions.

There are no limits to caring ®

October 29

And we know that God causes everything to work together for the good of those who love God and are called according to his purpose for them (Romans 8:28, NLT).

We'll See

In a small village lived a poor farmer. He used a horse to plow his field. One afternoon, his horse dropped dead. Everyone said it was a horrible thing, but the farmer replied, "We'll see."

He was so at peace, the village gave him a new horse. Now everyone thought he was a lucky man. The farmer replied, "We'll see."

A few days later, the new horse ran off. What a poor fellow, everyone thought. The farmer replied, "We'll see."

The horse finally returned and when he did, the farmer's son fell off while riding and broke his leg. The village thought what a shame, the farmer again said, "We'll see."

Two days later, the army came to draft new recruits. Seeing the son had a broken leg, they didn't recruit him.

Often, it's just too early to say if something is good or bad in our lives. We'll see!

There are no limits to caring ®

October 30

As for you, you meant evil against me, but God meant it for good... (Genesis 50:20, ESV).

Broken Places

In the book, *For Whom the Bell Tolls,* Ernest Hemmingway wrote, "Sooner or later life breaks everyone; and some emerge stronger in the broken places."

Today you have the opportunity to emerge stronger, better for the difficulties you have faced.

When a leg is broken, a cast is placed on the broken leg, and it heals and is stronger in the place that was broken.

When a piece of broken iron is welded together, it is the strongest at the point of brokenness.

We have been broken in many ways by powerful hurricanes: Ivan, Katrina, Laura, Sally. But depending on how we handled our brokenness, we had the possibility of becoming much stronger as a person or a community.

It is not the broken places that are the challenges, it how we handle the brokenness. Our response will make the difference. We can become bitter or better.

There are no limits to caring ®

October 31

Behold, children are a heritage from the Lord, the fruit of the womb a reward. Like arrows in the hand of a warrior are the children of one's youth. Blessed is the man who fills his quiver with them! He shall not be put to shame when he speaks with his enemies in the gate (Psalm 127:3-5, ESV).

Trick or Treat

Halloween is here, but some of you adults may be too old to go trick or treating.

You may be too old if:

1. you get winded from knocking on the door
2. you have to have another kid chew the candy for you
3. you ask for high fiber candy
4. when someone drops a candy bar in your bag, you lose your balance and fall over
5. when people compliment you on your mask, but you aren't wearing one
6. when the door opens you yell, "Trick, or…" and can't remember the rest
7. you have to carefully choose a costume that won't dislodge your hairpiece
8. you are the only Power Ranger in the neighborhood on a walker

It might be best to stay home and be nice to the kiddies who come to your door. Give yourself a rest, and the kids a treat.

There are no limits to caring ®

November 1

Charm is deceptive, and beauty does not last (Proverbs 31:30, NLT).

Reality

A woman rushed in to see her doctor, looking very worried. She said, "Doctor, take a look at me. I looked at myself in the mirror this morning and saw my hair all wiry and frazzled, my skin all wrinkled and pasty, my eyes blood-shot and bugging out, and this corpse-like look on my face! What's wrong with me doctor?"

The doctor looked her over for a couple of minutes, then calmly said, "Well, I can tell you one thing…there's nothing wrong with your eyesight."

If we can see ourselves as we are – there's nothing wrong with our eyesight. We may see the warts, but underneath the warts and wrinkles, there may be a heart of gold. A heart of compassion – a heart of caring – a heart of giving. That's where the real beauty lies.

What do you see when you look in the mirror? Surely more than wrinkles!

There are no limits to caring ®

November 2

*If one person falls, the other can reach out and help. But someone
who falls alone is in real trouble* (Ecclesiastes 4:10, NLT).

Challenged

A few years ago, at the Seattle Special Olympics, nine contestants, all physically or mentally challenged, assembled for the 100-yard dash. When the gun was shot, they all started out with a desire to run to the finish and win. However, one little boy stumbled on the asphalt, fell, and began to cry.

The other eight contestants heard the boy crying. They slowed down and looked back. Then they all turned around and went back...every one of them.

One girl bent down, kissed him, and said, "This will make it better." Then all nine linked arms and walked together to the finish line.

Everyone in the stadium stood and cheered. They understood what truly matters in this life more than winning for ourselves. What matters in this life is helping others win, even if it means slowing down and changing our course. A candle loses nothing by lighting another candle.

There are no limits to caring ®

November 3

Any kingdom divided against itself will be ruined, and a house divided against itself will fall (Luke 11:17, NIV).

Apathy

In 1787, Alexander Tyler, a history professor, wrote:
The average age of the world's greatest civilizations from the beginning of history has been about 200 years. During those 200 years, these nations always progressed through the following sequence:

- From bondage to spiritual faith;
- From spiritual faith to great courage;
- From courage to liberty;
- From liberty to abundance;
- From abundance to complacency;
- From complacency to apathy;
- From apathy to dependence;
- From dependence back into bondage.

So, where are we as a country?

- Voter turnout is apathetic;
- We want quick solutions to all our problems;
- We don't want to pay taxes, but we want all the services;
- Special interests are more important than the interest of the whole.

So, where are we? Divided and apathetic? If so, we are not far from bondage. Our future is only as bright as we are willing to sacrifice. And that's what scares me.

There are no limits to caring ®

November 4

Therefore encourage one another and build each other up, just as in fact you are doing. (1 Thessalonians 5:11, NLT).

Affirmation

Do you ever need a word of affirmation?

As I went to sit down after giving a speech, my grandson looked at me and gave me a thumbs up. That warmed my heart. It was affirmation.

When my two granddaughters come running to me with a hug, that's affirmation. When Leo, a family dog, gives affection, it is affirmation.

When my wife gives me words of encouragement and validation, that's affirmation that I need.

From our family, we learn the importance of affirming one another. But in the real world, affirmation is not always readily given.

The number one reason why an employee leaves a job is a lack of affirmation. Affirming one another fills our tank. Who can you affirm today?

November 5

It is better to heed the rebuke of a wise person than to listen to the song of fools (Ecclesiastes 7:5, NIV).

Great Marriages

A couple was celebrating their golden wedding anniversary; they had long been the talk of the town.

A local newspaper reporter was inquiring as to the secret of their marriage. "It dates back to our honeymoon," explained the man. "We visited the Grand Canyon and took a trip on pack mules. We hadn't gone too far when my wife's mule stumbled. My wife said, "That's once.""

We proceeded a little further and the mule stumbled again. My wife said, "That's twice." We hadn't gone far when the mule stumbled the third time. My wife removed a revolver from her purse and shot the mule dead. I started to protest, when she looked at me, and quietly said, "That's once."

"And we lived happily ever after." There's always a reason for a great marriage. The wife says what she means, and the husband listens carefully. That's the beginning of a great marriage.

There are no limits to caring ®

November 6

Do your best to present yourself to God as one approved, a worker who has no need to be ashamed, rightly handling the word of truth (2 Timothy 2:15, ESV).

Buddy

A man was driving along a rural road and accidentally drove his car into a ditch. Luckily, a local farmer offered to help pull the man's car out by hitching up his horse named Buddy. The farmer hitched Buddy up to the car and yelled, "Pull, Nellie, pull!" Buddy didn't move. Then the farmer shouted, "Pull, Buster, pull!" Buddy didn't respond. Once more the farmer commanded, "Pull, Coco, pull!" Still nothing.

Then the farmer said, "Pull, Buddy, pull!" And the horse easily dragged the car out of the ditch. The motorist was very curious. He asked the farmer why he called his horse by the wrong name three times. The farmer replied, "Buddy is blind and if he thought he was the only one pulling, he wouldn't even try!"

It's not enough to wait for the crowd to come join you before you do the right thing. Doing what you are called to do may mean doing it alone. Don't wait, just do it.

November 7

Many waters cannot quench love, neither can floods drown it
(Song of Solomon 8:7, ESV).

Looking for Love

The following ad appeared in a newspaper…

"Single female…seeks male companionship. I'm a very good-looking girl who LOVES to play. I love long walks in the woods, riding in your pickup truck, hunting, camping, fishing trips, and cozy winter nights lying by the fire. Candlelight dinners will have me eating out of your hand. Rub me the right way and watch me respond. I'll be at the front door when you get home from work, wearing only what nature gave me. Kiss me, and I'm yours. Call 555-1529 and ask for Daisy."

15,000 men responded to the ad and found themselves talking to the local humane society about an 8-week old Labrador Retriever.

Some of you men fail to realize that what you are looking for is at your own back door. See the possibilities in your own spouse. It's a doggone good place to start.

November 8

*I have also seen this example of wisdom under the sun, and it
seemed great to me* (Ecclesiastes 9:13, ESV).

A Dog's Teachings

If dogs were teachers, we would learn things like:

- When loved ones come home, always run to greet them.
- Never pass up the opportunity to go for a joyride.
- Take naps.
- Stretch before rising.
- Run and play daily.
- Avoid biting when a simple growl will do.
- On warm days, stop to lie on your back on the grass.
- On hot days, drink lots of water and lie under a shady tree.
- Eat with gusto, stop when you've had enough.
- When you're happy, dance around and wag your entire body.
- Delight in the simple joy of a long walk.
- Be Loyal. Never pretend to be something you're not.
- If what you want lies buried, dig until you find it.
- When someone is having a bad day, be silent, sit close by and
nuzzle them gently.

Maybe it is a dog's world after all.

There are no limits to caring ®

November 9

The LORD is near to the brokenhearted and saves the crushed in spirit (Psalm 34:18, ESV).

Grief

Young Robin contracted leukemia and battled the disease for seven painful months. Robin died, and her parents, Barbara and George, were extremely depressed. The pain became intense and kept the parents awake at night. Nothing would make the pain go away.

The seven-year-old younger George took on the job as cheerleader for his parents. He would tell stories, jokes, or act silly to cheer up his parents – to see their smiling faces – anything to remove the dark spirit of depression.

One day, Barbara overheard her young son George tell a child, "I can't come out and play because my mother needs me."

That was the beginning of the cure for Barbara's depression. She realized that she must resolve her own grief, and that her seven-year-old son must first be a child.

Barbara said, "I realized I was too much of a burden for a little seven-year-old boy to carry."

Each of us must deal with our own stuff and not pass it on to our children. By the way, this young George became the forty-third president of the United States.

There are no limits to caring ®

November 10

Never give up. Eagerly follow the Holy Spirit and serve the Lord
(Romans 12:11, CEV).

Lincoln Failure

Many times, we lose our courage in facing life because of past failures or fear of failure. Abraham Lincoln knew what it meant to fail, but his defeats didn't stop him. He is an example of the successful use of defeat to achieve victory. Abraham Lincoln's record is as follows:

- Lost job
- Failed in business
- His Sweetheart died
- Had nervous breakdown
- Defeated for nomination for Congress
- Elected to Congress
- Lost re-nomination
- Defeated for Senate
- Defeated for nomination for Vice-President
- Defeated for Senate
- Elected President

Lincoln pushed on in the face of difficulties and failures that would have discouraged most of us.

Our defeats don't have to defeat us. We can find victory out of our defeats if we don't give up. We must never give up!

We can learn to say: "With God's help I shall not fail."

There are no limits to caring ®

November 11

The God who equipped me with strength . . . He made my feet like the feet of a deer and set me secure on the heights. He trains my hands for war, so that my arms can bend a bow of bronze (Psalm 18:32-34, ESV).

Veterans Day

We celebrate Veteran's Day today. We honor those who have served our country... with courage and sacrifice. Today, we have over 21 million veterans. We pause to give thanks for their great service. We each know a veteran.

My dad was a veteran who was drafted during World War II and re-enlisted and served in the Korean War. And my brother-in-law served in the Gulf War. And my son served in Afghanistan and Iraq.

Today is time for each of us to thank those who have served as a military person for our county. It could be your family, friends or co-worker.

To our Veteran... on behalf of each of us... we say "thank you for your service," and to your family, "thank you for the sacrifice you made while our country was being protected by your loved one." THANK YOU!

Go and express your gratitude for veterans you know!

There are no limits to caring ®

November 12

*So then let us pursue what makes for peace and for mutual
upbuilding*
(Romans 14:19, ESV).

Owl

Two taxidermists stopped to look at an owl on display in a store window. They immediately began to criticize the way it was mounted. The eyes didn't look natural. The wings weren't set properly. And the feathers were not neatly arranged. When they had finished with their criticism and were about to move on, the owl moved his head and winked at them!

Most critics like to think of themselves as experts. The truth is, it doesn't take much ability to be a critic. In fact, it's usually pretty easy to spot flaws and weaknesses, especially in other people! But, as in the case of the taxidermists, even the experts can be wrong at times!

It's sometimes more difficult to look for things to compliment, for things to praise. We can either be known as critics or encouragers! Go for the encouragement…the world already has enough critics!

November 13

Kiss me and kiss me again, for your love is sweeter than wine
(Song of Songs 1:2, NLT).

All Tied Up

A schoolteacher in Oklahoma was desperate to bring passion back into his marriage. So, he devised a plan that would make him look like a knight in shining armor.

He hired two of his students to break into his home and tie up his wife. His plan included his heroic rescue of his wife and a choreographed fight with the students. He was sure his plan would work.

The night for the break-in came and all was going well, until his wife escaped and phoned the police.

The police arrived to discover that the break-in was fake.

Maybe your marriage needs a little spark in it – but there's a better way. Do something special. Don't wait for your mate to tie you up.

That kind of investment will keep the fires burning and your spouse will know that you not only love in words, but also in deed.

There are no limits to caring ®

November 14

Do not withhold good from those who deserve it when it's in your power to help them (Proverbs 3:27, NLT).

Anna and Joe

Back in 2005, Mike was driving on the interstate near Tennessee, when an accident caused traffic to come to a standstill. Drivers and passengers parked their vehicles and stretched their legs.

Several stood around Mike's truck, complaining about the inconvenience and wishing for something to eat and drink.

An elderly couple, Anna and Joe, were in a loaded-down pickup truck nearby and happily offered everyone a soda and some sandwiches.

Noticing that Anna and Joe had a Mississippi tag and remembering that Hurricane Katrina had just hit Mississippi, Mike inquired if the hurricane had affected them. Joe said, "We lost everything except what you see in our pickup."

Anna and Joe were traveling to their son's home in Virginia to start over. Everyone offered to pay Anna and Joe for the food, but they replied, "It's better to give than to receive." Anna and Joe lost almost everything they owned, and yet they were happy to give what they had-- to some weary travelers, and they expected nothing in return.

There are no limits to caring ®

November 15

Be friendly with everyone. Don't be proud and feel that you know more than others. Make friends with ordinary people (Romans 12:16, CEV).

Dolphins

Four lifeguards were swimming near the coastline at Ocean Beach in New Zealand, when suddenly a group of dolphins swam up and began swimming around, encircling them.

The lifeguards were startled and confused by the dolphins' strange behavior. It seemed that the dolphins were trying to herd them together.

When one of the lifeguards tried to drift away from the group, two of the dolphins herded him back – just as he spotted a nine-foot, great white shark heading toward him.

The dolphins were defending them from a shark attack! Moments later they swam away, and the lifeguards made it ashore …unharmed.

We are stronger when we are surrounded by our friends and family, by those that care for us. When we are isolated, we endanger ourselves.

Don't live in isolation. Too busy for friends or even your family? You need a friend and you need to be a friend. Reach out to those around you and especially your family.

There are no limits to caring ®

November 16

My son, if sinful men entice you, do not give in to them (Proverbs 1:10, NIV).

Crab

A certain crab trap is designed to catch even the smartest of crabs. It's a wire cage with a hole at the top. Bait is placed inside, and the cage is lowered into the water. Soon, a crab enters the cage and begins eating the bait.

A second crab joins. Soon more crabs come along -- long after the bait is gone.

Should one of the crabs try to leave, the others will gang up on it and repeatedly pull it back down. If it's persistent, they will tear off its claws or even kill it.

The crabs -- by force of the majority -- stay together in the cage. The cage is hauled up, and it's dinnertime on the pier.

When you have a dream, don't allow yourself to be pulled down by those around you. And for goodness sake, don't pull down those around you!

See dreams become reality.

November 17

Never let loyalty and kindness leave you! Tie them around your neck as a reminder…. Then, you will find favor with both God and people (Proverbs 3:3-4, NLT).

Hotel

One stormy night, an elderly couple entered the lobby of a hotel in Philadelphia. Trying to get out of the rain, they asked for a room. But all the rooms were booked. Unwilling to turn them away, the clerk offered his room to the couple.

The next morning, they checked out and thanked the clerk for his kindness.

A year later, the clerk received a letter from the elderly couple. It enclosed a round-trip ticket to New York, inviting him to visit.

The elderly man met him in New York and led him to a brand new, magnificent hotel on Fifth Avenue. With a smile, the elderly man asked the clerk if he would like to become the manager of the new hotel.

The elderly man's name was William Waldorf Astor, and the magnificent hotel was the original Waldorf-Astoria Hotel.

Those who treat others with kindness and respect will be treated likewise.

There are no limits to caring ®

November 18

One who is wise is cautious and turns away from evil, but a fool is reckless and careless (Proverbs 14:16, ESV).

Three Wives

When you are in the hospital, you may receive balloons, or flowers or a card. But when a certain man woke from his surgery, he found no flowers, only his three wives.

Recently a man in London had been admitted to the hospital for a triple bypass operation. His three wives had come to the hospital to visit him. To their surprise, they soon realized that they all were married to the same man! His complicated marital affairs took a turn for the worse.

No matter how complicated or wonderful your marriage is, lack of communication is never a good thing. Honesty is vital to a healthy relationship.

Maybe it's time you and your spouse take that long-awaited romantic getaway together. Or maybe a date night this weekend. Whatever it takes, spend time together, talking and listening—and you will never have big surprises.

November 19

Life is not measured by how much you own (Luke 12:15, NLT).

How Poor We Are

A wealthy man took his son to the country to show him how poor people lived. After a few days living with a farm family, the father asked the son, "What did you learn about how poor people live?"

The boy said, "I learned that we have one dog, and they have four. We have a pool that reaches across our yard; they have a creek that goes on forever. We have a small piece of land to live on, and they have fields that go beyond our sight. We buy our food; they grow their own." The son added, "Thanks, Dad, for showing me just how poor we are."

Often, we forget what we have and focus on what we don't have. It is all a matter of perspective. As we come to this time of the year, it's time to count blessings and be grateful.

There are no limits to caring ®

November 20

Above all, keep loving one another earnestly . . . (1 Peter 4:8, ESV).

Dungy

Coach Tony Dungy's eighteen-year- old son committed suicide near the end of the 2005 football season. At the funeral service, Coach Dungy, head coach of the Indianapolis Colts at the time, offered a heartbreaking appeal to fathers.

"God can provide joy in the midst of a sad occasion," he said. "The challenge is to find that joy. I urge you not to take your relationships for granted. Parents, hug your kids each chance you get. Tell them you love them, each chance you get. You don't know when it's going to be the last time."

Tony Dungy last saw his son at Thanksgiving when his son was in a rush to get to the airport, and his father did not have a chance to hug him.

Our children, no matter the age, need parents to hug them – to love them, no matter the circumstances. Life is tough.

There are no limits to caring ®

November 21

Rescue the weak and the needy; deliver them from the hand of the wicked
(Psalm 82:4, ESV).

Circle of Friends

In Africa, a 12-year-old girl had been missing for nearly a week. Police and relatives searched for her. They all feared the worst.

When she was found on the outskirts of the town, the rescue team had discovered something remarkably strange. Lions were standing guard over her. As the rescuers began to approach, the lions simply left her—like a gift—and went back into the forest!

She had been taken and beaten repeatedly by seven men. If the lions had not come to her rescue, then it could have been much worse.

Just as the lions watched over the little girl, it is our responsibility to look out for those in need. Those who have been beaten down by life. Those who find themselves in a hopeless situation. Those who need a circle of strong friends. You can be that strong friend!

There are no limits to caring ®

November 22

Then Peter came to Jesus and asked, "Lord, how many times shall I forgive my brother…? Up to seven times?" Jesus answered, "I tell you, not seven times, but seventy-seven times" (Matthew 18:21-22, NIV).

Thanksgiving Pardon

A football team had just finished their daily practice session when a large turkey came strutting onto the field. The turkey walked right up to the head coach and demanded a tryout. The players stopped what they were doing and watched in amazement.

Everyone stared in astonishment as the turkey caught pass after pass and ran right through the defensive line. After the tryout was over, the turkey sat down on the sidelines. The coach shouted, "You're terrific! You will definitely be playing on *this* team for the season." The turkey replied, "Before I commit for the season…All I want to know is, does the season go past Thanksgiving Day?"

Each year, the president pardons one lucky turkey from being sent to the Thanksgiving dinner table. This Thanksgiving, maybe someone needs your pardon. Your forgiveness. Maybe it's a family member, a friend, or even a co-worker.

This Thanksgiving, extend forgiveness.

There are no limits to caring ®

November 23

A good name is better than precious ointment... (Ecclesiastes 7:1, ESV).

Nobel

One morning Alfred Nobel, the inventor of dynamite, awoke to read his own obituary. Actually, his brother had died, and the reporter carelessly reported the death of the wrong brother.

The obituary stated, "The merchant of death is dead!" It went on to say, "Dr. Alfred Nobel, who became rich by finding ways to kill more people faster than ever before, died yesterday."

Alfred was shocked as he read the obituary, because he saw himself as the world saw him. He resolved to make clear to the world the true purpose of his life.

Nobel signed his last will and testament and set aside the bulk of his estate to create the Five Nobel Prizes for outstanding contributions in physics, chemistry, medicine, and literature. The fifth is for peace, known as the "Nobel Peace Prize."

Today is your day to make clear to the world the true purpose of your life. What impression will you leave today?

There are no limits to caring ®

November 24

Come now, you who say, "Today or tomorrow we will go into such and such a town and spend a year there and trade and make a profit"—yet you do not know what tomorrow will bring. What is your life? For you are a mist that appears for a little time and then vanishes (James 4:13-14, ESV).

Dash of Life

I recently visited the gravesite of my grandmother. On the tombstone was her birth date, November 24, 1906, and then her death date, December 25, 1987. In between these two dates was a dash, not very long – but that represented her life – between the beginning and the ending.

In that dash, she was a good person, she worked hard, faithful to her family, church and community. In that dash, she made a difference to the people around her. She was loving, kind, and what every kid wants in a grandmother. All was done in the dash.

As you think about your own tombstone, your birth date may be fixed, but you are living in the dash, now. What you do today – for other people – will have a lasting impact. Today is your dash of life. Make the most of it.

There are no limits to caring ®

November 25

Let everyone be quick to hear [be a careful, thoughtful listener],
slow to speak [a speaker of carefully chosen words and], slow to
anger [patient, reflective, forgiving] (James 1:19, AMP).

Communication

Marriage experts tell us that the number one cause for divorce in America today is a lack of communication. That's sad, because almost everyone is born with one mouth and two ears – the basic tools for communication. But, possessing the physical tools of communication is not enough. Couples need to learn how to use the mouth and ears for communication to take place.

Someone offered a good rule of thumb. "Because there are two ears and one mouth, we ought to spend twice as much time listening as we do talking." Good advice. Learning to hear what a person is really saying is a key to good communication. Just being willing to listen to your mate is an indication of respect and shows that you care.

Today is a good day to practice listening. Learning to listen to each other and then talking *WITH*, not *AT*, them will pay rich dividends.

There are no limits to caring ®

November 26

Doing wrong is fun for a fool, but living wisely brings pleasure to the sensible (Proverbs 10:23, NLT).

Cool Mom

In Colorado, a mother pled guilty to felony charges for supplying drugs and alcohol to minors. This group of minors consisted of her son and several of his friends.

Why would a mother supply illegal drugs and alcohol to her own child? Because she wanted to be a "cool mom." The mother told police that she had not been popular in high school, and she was now feeling "like one of the group."

Times have changed. When a mother feels that it's more important to be cool than to be concerned for the welfare of her child.

As parents, we ask ourselves "What does it really mean to love our children?"

- To give them whatever they want?
- To have no expectations?

That may make us pretty cool in their eyes—but it's not love.

Parenting isn't about the parent's need, but about what's good for the child.

November 27

Each of you should use whatever gift you have received to serve others, as faithful stewards of God's grace in its various forms (1 Peter 4:10, NIV).

Church Goers

In 2005, on the first Sunday morning after Hurricane Katrina, about 250 worshipers attended the church service in a storm-damaged church in Gulfport, Mississippi. There was no air conditioning, and the only light came from the large hole in the roof.

Dressed in mismatched clothes received from a donation site, the pastor made a profound statement:

"The day of church as we know it is over."

At the close of the service, loads of food and water arrived at the church parking lot, sent from concerned people all over the country. By Sunday afternoon, church members and other volunteers were distributing the much-needed supplies to the community.

The church members learned an important lesson that day. They learned that church is not just about sitting in a pew on Sunday and listening to the preacher. Church is about people – people reaching out and serving those in need, loving one another as they love themselves – that is what the church is.

Church as usual? No. Church as it should be? Yes.

There are no limits to caring ®

November 28

So be strong and courageous! Do not be afraid and do not panic before them. For the LORD your God will personally go ahead of you. He will neither fail you nor abandon you (Deuteronomy 31:6, NLT).

Strength and Courage

In order to face difficult and trying times, both the qualities of strength and courage are needed. There is a difference between the two.

- It takes strength to endure abuse. It takes courage to stop it.
- It takes strength to stand alone. It takes courage to lean on another.
- It takes strength to love. It takes courage to be loved.
- It takes strength to survive. It takes courage to live.

In this world, we need both strength and courage in order to deal effectively with our troubles. We need the strength to stand up to the trials and the courage to go on with our lives, enjoying the freedoms and liberties this great land offers us.

Strength and courage are the qualities that defined those who established our nation and fought to make it great. May the same be said of this present generation.

There are no limits to caring ®

November 29

Love never fails (1 Corinthians 13:8, NIV).

Brother's Love

An expectant mother helped her three-year-old son prepare for the birth of his baby sister. She let him sing to the baby in her womb each night, "You are my sunshine…".

The delivery was complicated, and the baby girl was rushed to a neonatal intensive care unit, where her condition deteriorated. With the baby near the point of death, the little brother begged to see and sing to his sister.

As he began to sing, "You are my sunshine, my only sunshine…" the baby's breathing and heart rate started improving.

The longer he sang, "You are my sunshine…please don't take my sunshine away," the better the baby got until, finally, she stabilized.

The medical staff called it a miracle. The mother called it a miracle of a brother's love. Others called it a miracle of God's love. What would you call it?

There are no limits to caring ®

November 30

I have always tried my best to let wisdom guide my thoughts and actions. I said to myself, "I am determined to be wise." But it didn't work (Ecclesiastes 7:23, NLT).

Grandpa's Wisdom

Listen to these words of wisdom about marriage, from Grandpa:

- Whether a man winds up with a nest egg or a goose egg depends on the kind of chick he marries.
- Too many couples marry for better or worse, but not for good.
- When a man marries a woman, they become one, but the trouble starts when they try to decide which one.
- If a man has enough "horse sense" to treat his wife like a thoroughbred, she will never be an old nag.
- On anniversaries, the wise husband always forgets the past...but never the present.

Sounds like grandpa was a wise man, but then he blew it. Grandpappy and his wife were discussing their 50th wedding anniversary, when she said, "Shall I kill a chicken to celebrate?" "Naw," said Grandpappy, "Why blame a bird for something that happened 50 years ago?"

There are no limits to caring ®

December 1

*Listen to advice and accept instruction, that you may gain wisdom
in the future* (Proverbs 19:10, ESV).

Listening

A man asked his wife what she'd like for her birthday. "I'd love to be six again," she replied. On the morning of her birthday, he got her up early and took her to the local theme park. He insisted that she ride every ride—the roller coaster, the screaming loop, the Death Slide. Five hours later, she staggered out of the park with her stomach upside down. He then took her to McDonald's, where he ordered a happy meal with a chocolate shake. Then, off to the movies where he insisted she have popcorn, a hot dog, and candy.

Finally, she wobbled home and collapsed into bed. He leaned over and gently said, "Well, dear, how did you like being six again?"

"You idiot, I meant my dress size."

Some men can't get it right, even when their heart is right.

Listen carefully to your wife. She may not say what you hear.

There are no limits to caring ®

December 2

*And whatever you do, in word or deed, do everything in the name
of the Lord Jesus, giving thanks to God the Father through him*
(Colossians 3:17, ESV).

Starfish

A man was walking along the beach, when he noticed a boy picking up starfish and gently throwing them into the ocean.

Curious, the man approached the boy and asked, "What are you doing?"

The boy answered, "If I don't throw these starfish back, they'll die."

The man replied, "There are miles and miles of beach and hundreds of starfish. You can't possibly make a difference!"

The boy picked up another starfish and threw it into the surf. Then, smiling at the man, he said, "I made a difference for that one."

Our nation is facing overwhelming troubles and strife. The needs are great. At VOA, one by one, we are making a difference.

Hundreds of volunteers are working with us. Tens of thousands of dollars and goods are donated. These goods are distributed directly and quickly to those in need. We don't have red tape to cut through. We just do it.

The needs are great, we'll do one starfish at a time and so can you. Join us.

There are no limits to caring ®

December 3

So be wise as serpents and innocent as doves (Matthew 10:16, ESV).

Careful

A pastor I know left the pulpit area during the musical part of the worship service to close a door and adjust the thermostat. He then disappeared for a few minutes. After the music ended, coming over the sound system was the sound of a toilet flushing, water running, and the tearing of a paper towel.

The pastor apparently had forgotten he was wearing a wireless microphone. When he came back in the sanctuary, he found the entire congregation doubled over with laughter. He had no idea why they were laughing, until someone told him. At that moment, he would rather have been somewhere else!

At times, we all want to be somewhere else, but unfortunately, we have to be where we are – where people see and hear what we do and say. That should make us all want to do and say the right thing. You never know who's watching or listening.

December 4

No discipline is enjoyable while it is happening—it's painful! But afterward there will be a peaceful harvest of right living for those who are trained in this way (Hebrews 12:11, NLT).

Shortcuts

Ever taken a shortcut? The other day, I took a shortcut. I was supposed to save 20 miles, but the shortcut turned into a LONG cut! I got lost and wasted time trying to get back on the main road.

Sometimes in life, we take shortcuts that don't take us anywhere. In life, there are no real shortcuts. They may advertise, "Lose weight with no exercise! Just take a pill!" But there is no shortcut to a healthy lifestyle. It requires healthy food and exercise.

Sometimes, we want to take a shortcut – skip academic preparation for life. Or, maybe take a shortcut to a good marriage. But academic shortcuts do not prepare us for life, and shortcuts in a marriage do not bring about intimate relationships.

There are no shortcuts to happiness. Happiness is a by-product of giving and not taking. When we pay the full price and travel down the main road, we usually get where we need to be.

There are no limits to caring ®

December 5

There were giants in the earth in those days (Genesis 6:4, KJV).

Greatest Generation

Many people have questioned whether or not this present generation has what it takes to tackle the challenges of a hostile world.

Tom Brokaw wrote the book, *The Greatest Generation.* He identified those who fought in WWII, came back home, and built this country to what it is – the greatest generation of all time. It was the times that made the generation great. The problem is, that generation is dying off.

What about today's generation? Maybe we get a glimpse of who we are in those New York firemen and policemen who sacrificed everything. Or the passengers on Flight 93 who took on those hijackers. Or the 50% increase in young recruits for our armed forces. Or the $150 million raised for the victims' families in one night. Maybe that's a glimpse of who we are.

There are no limits to caring ®

December 6

But Noah found favor in the eyes of the LORD (Genesis 6:8, ESV).

Noah

Noah was told to build an Ark. What's an Ark? No one had ever built one before, but Noah did as he was instructed. He built it years before he was to use it. When it was ready, it just sat there. He couldn't launch it. However, the water finally came to him and lifted his Ark, his family, and all the animals.

So it is with us. We live as we are taught; we raise our family as they should be. We teach them the right values for life and point them in a divine direction and hope they are ready for the storms to come. It is those circumstances that test how we are built.

We may know more about smooth sailing, but smooth sailing doesn't build character. The coming days are opportunities for building character and defining who we are. And, with God's help, we will have the grace for facing these challenging days.

There are no limits to caring ®

December 7

In this world you will have tribulation. But take heart; I have overcome the world (John 16:33, ESV).

Getting Ready for Difficult Days

As a country, we've had some difficult days. I am convinced many more difficult days are coming our way, as a nation. How do we get ready?

When we do it right, we learn one day at time. Each day as we learn, we gain strength, confidence, and wisdom for the next day.

It is not in the calm waters that the sailor learns to master the sea. It is during the storms that he learns to master his skills. And, so it is with life. We may never know our strength until we face the test. The real test for a new ship is in the water, the real test for an airplane is in the air, the real test for a quarterback is on the football field, and the real test for us will be how we live as a nation in crisis.

We can say we care, but only in testing can we demonstrate, there are no limits to caring.

There are no limits to caring ®

December 8

*One person gives freely, yet gains even more; another withholds
unduly, but comes to poverty* (Proverbs 11:24, NIV).

A King's Burden

A king had twin sons, Joseph and George, and sought to
designate one of them as his successor.

One day, he said to them, "The burdens of sovereignty are heavy.
To determine which of you is better able to bear them, I will place
equal burdens on your shoulders and send you to a far corner of the
kingdom. Whoever returns first, bearing his burden like a king,
will be my successor.

The brothers set out together. Soon, they came upon an elderly
woman struggling under a heavy burden. Joseph suggested they
stop to help her. George protested: "We have a burden of our
own". And so, he hurried on.

Joseph stayed behind and eventually arrived at the palace. George
had arrived first, but without his burden. George exclaimed, "The
burden was too heavy for me. How did you do it?" Joseph, the
future king replied, "When I helped others carry their burdens, I
found strength to carry my own."

There are no limits to caring ®

December 9

*Be on your guard; stand firm in the faith; be men of courage; be
strong* (1 Corinthians 16:13, NIV).

Hero

Butch O'Hare was a pilot on the aircraft carrier Lexington, in
World War II. One day, his squadron was sent on a mission,
but because his plane was not fueled properly, he had to return to
the carrier. On his way back, he discovered a squadron of Japanese
bombers on their way to attack the American fleet. He gunned
down five enemy bombers before he ran out of ammunition. He
then darted in and out among them, until they diverted their course.

He became the Navy's first Ace of the war. He was awarded the
Congressional Medal of Honor. A year later, he was killed in
combat at the age of 29. His hometown of Chicago named O'Hare
Airport in his honor.

Courage ran in Butch's family. His father was Easy Eddy, the mob
lawyer who testified against Al Capone, in order to secure a good
name to give to his son.

There are no limits to caring ®

December 10

Greater love has no one than this, that someone lay down his life for his friends (John 15:13, ESV).

The Rest of the Story

Easy Eddie was a lawyer for Chicago Mob Boss Al Capone. His skill as a lawyer kept Capone out of jail for a long time, and he was paid well for his services. He lived the high life and enjoyed all the benefits of wealth.

But Eddie had a young son he adored. He wanted to teach the child right from wrong, but he had a problem with his own reputation. He couldn't give his son a good name because of his mob connections. So, he decided to come clean and testify against the mob.

He knew that he risked everything by breaking the code of silence. His love and concern for his son indeed did cost him everything. Within a year, he was gunned down in the streets of Chicago.

He made the ultimate sacrifice in order to finally secure a good name for the sake of his son. What sacrifices are you making for your children? Proverbs 22:1 says, *"A good name is more desirable than great riches"*.

There are no limits to caring ®

December 11

*Let what you say be simply "Yes" or "No," anything more than
this comes from evil* (Matthew 5:37, ESV).

Yes or No

During a flight on a small airline, the flight attendant asked a
passenger if he would like to have dinner.

"What are my choices?" the passenger asked.

"Yes or no," the flight attendant replied.

Wouldn't it be great if all the great choices in life came down to a
simple "yes" or "no"? Perhaps they do.

Are you going to work today? Yes, or no?
Are you going to give your best? Yes, or no?
Are you going to keep a promise? Yes, or no?
Are you going to be faithful to your spouse? Yes, or no?
Are you going to live a self-centered life? Yes, or no.

It all eventually comes down to a "yes" or "no." We may not be
able to determine the circumstances in our lives, but we will answer
yes or no to whatever life brings our way.

There are no limits to caring ®

December 12

Woe to you, teachers of the law and Pharisees, you hypocrites!
You give a tenth of your spices.... But you have neglected the
more important matters of the law—justice, mercy and
faithfulness... You blind guides! You strain out a gnat but
swallow a camel (Matthew 23:23-24, NIV).

Lone Ranger and Tonto

The Lone Ranger and Tonto camped in the desert. They set up their tent and fell asleep. Later, the Lone Ranger woke Tonto and said, "Tonto, look at the sky and tell me what you see." Tonto replied, "Millions of stars." "What does that tell you?" asked the Lone Ranger. Tonto said, "Astronomically speaking, it tells me there are millions of galaxies and potentially billions of planets. Astrologically, it tells me that Saturn is in Leo. Theologically, it's evident the Lord is all powerful and we are small and insignificant. What does it tell you, Kemosabe?"

The Lone Ranger said, "It tells me someone has stolen our tent!"

Sometimes we "get stars in our eyes" and fail to miss the tent – that which provides a covering of love and protection. More than the glitter of the stars, we need the security of family, and caring relationships.

December 13

But you are a chosen people, a royal priesthood, a holy nation,
God's special possession, that you may declare the praises of him
who called you out of darkness into his wonderful light.
(1 Peter 2:9, NLT).

Treasure

A mother told her young son that the vase up on the mantle was from her grandparents, a beloved treasure. He knew not to touch it.

But somehow, he found a way to touch it. He wasn't trying to be bad. He just wanted to see if the tiny rose border went all around the back. He was just curious.

And he didn't mean to drop it.

It shattered to the floor, and he began to cry. That cry quickly grew louder, as his mom came into the room.

Her son could barely get out the words, "I broke the vase." With a look of relief, she said, "Oh thank heavens. I thought you were hurt!"

She made it clear to the child that *he* was the real treasure.

Things do have value, but people are priceless. Never forget what really counts in life. A shattered vase or a shattered heart; remember to show mercy.

There are no limits to caring ®

December 14

You must encourage one another each day... (Hebrews 3:13, CEV).

Helping Hand

Ruth Simmons is one of the great success stories of our day. Born in a sharecropper's shack in East Texas, Ruth became president of Brown University. She was the first African-American to head an Ivy League University.

As a child, Ruth lived in dire poverty. Her family had no TV, radio, or books. She looked forward to starting school so she could just have a pencil and paper. About her first teacher, Ida Mae Henderson, Ruth Simmons said, "She loved us, she inspired us. She started me believing I could do anything."

Dr. Simmons earned her Ph.D. from Harvard. She credits her teachers with her success. People believed in her, and she was empowered to believe in herself.

People who care do change lives. Look around you. There is someone who needs you to believe in them.

There are no limits to caring ®

December 15

The generous will prosper; those who refresh others will themselves be refreshed (Proverbs 11:25, NLT).

A Brother Like That

A man was showing his new car to his neighbors, when a boy walked up and voiced his admiration for the vehicle. He said, "I sure wish I had a car like this." The man said the car was a gift from his brother.

The young boy shook his head in amazement and started saying, "Gee, I sure wish…" Everyone present thought they knew exactly how he would finish, he would say, "Gee, I sure wish I had a brother like that." But what he said was, "Gee, I sure wish I could be a brother like that."

The man was shocked. He asked the boy why he would say that. The boy said, "I have a younger brother who is crippled. I would give anything to be able to say to him, 'This is your car, and I'll drive you wherever you want to go'."

In this Christmas season, ask yourself, "Do I want to have? Or do I want to be…?"

December 16

*Blessed is the one who considers the poor! In the day of trouble,
the LORD delivers him* (Psalm 41:1, ESV).

Santa Claus

Santa Claus is coming to town (very soon)! That's very big news. Children everywhere are excited about receiving gifts.

However, without your generosity, many would have no hope of a Christmas gift.

- A little boy will ride a bicycle Christmas day because a lady and her ten cousins sponsored a family.

- A young boy is receiving a microscope because a team of students at a local middle school sponsored his dream.

- A family, whose house burned, will have gifts under the Christmas tree because employees from a local company made it happen.

- A little boy who had nothing brought a can of peas to school to participate in giving to those less fortunate, but he will also ride a bicycle because a group of employees was touched by his generosity.

As we grow older, we learn that giving brings more joy than getting. May this Christmas season bring you the joy of giving.

There are no limits to caring ®

December 17

Give generously to the poor, not grudgingly, for the LORD your
God will bless you in everything you do
(Deuteronomy 15:10, NLT).

Children's Gifts

I'll Be Home for Christmas!" Remember that song? Unfortunately, too many children in our community have no hope of going home. Through no fault of their own, they are not living with their parents. And they won't be home for Christmas.

However, because of the generosity of hundreds of people through VOA in our community, over 2000 children will have a special Christmas gift...more than a toy... a message of hope and love, even in their darkest storm.

When I was a child, we didn't have much. I will never forget the kindness of our church. We gathered around an old wood heater in the church and received gifts that the church members had gotten for us...toys, trucks and dolls. My heart to this day is warmed by the memory of the kindness of those people...and the memory of that warm heater on that cold December night.

A little kindness can last a lifetime. Your generous heart and compassion can lead you to many children who need a little kindness this Christmas.

There are no limits to caring ®

December 18

*In the desert the whole community grumbled... The Israelites said
to them, "If only we had died by the LORD's hand in Egypt!
There we sat around pots of met and ate all the food we wanted,
but you have brought us out into this desert to starve this entire
assembly to death* (Exodus 16:2-3, NIV).

Cowboy

A young boy dreamed of being a cowboy and asked his father
for a horse for Christmas. This was the boy's only desire and
the only way he thought he could live out his dream of becoming a
cowboy.

Christmas Day came, and the little boy began opening his presents.
First, a slingshot, then a cap gun, and finally a pair of cowboy
boots. In a tantrum, the boy exclaimed, "How am I going to be a
cowboy if I don't even have a horse?!"

All the while, his father had a horse tied up in the backyard, waiting
for his son. The little boy, feeling a little bit foolish, did get his
horse and went on to become a cowboy!

Oftentimes, this is how we treat our Heavenly Father. We
complain, when all along, our gift or breakthrough from Him is
right around the corner. Trust God and know that He has the best
prepared for you!

December 19

Pure and genuine religion in the sight of God the Father means caring for orphans and widows in their distress and refusing to let the world corrupt you
(James 1:27, NLT).

Our Wish List

What's your wish this Christmas…a leather jacket, diamond earrings? What about a self-driving car like a Tesla – pretty neat, huh? What if I told you there were hundreds of people, right here in your community, who wish just for a hot meal to eat on Christmas?

What if I told you there were children, right here in your community, who will be lucky to get one used toy for Christmas? What if I told you there were elderly citizens in your community, who may spend Christmas alone, without even a Christmas card?

My wish for this Christmas is that you will partner with VOA and respond to these needs in your community. If not us, then partner with another organization dedicated to helping people in need. You see it's not so much about us; it's about helping others. Please call VOA or another local organization to see how you can help.

There are no limits to caring ®

December 20

Why, my soul, are you downcast? Why so disturbed within me?
Put your hope in God, for I will yet praise him, my Savior and my
God (Psalm 42:5, NIV).

Holiday Blues

Do you ever have the holiday blues… a time when you feel sad, lonely, or depressed? It is not uncommon for us to have these feelings during the holidays. For most, it is a season of happiness, but not for everyone.

If you are experiencing grief, financial difficulties, failing health, or unfulfilled dreams, all of the Christmas carols, decorations, and parties provide painful reminders of what might have been.

Here's what you can do to overcome the holiday blues:

- Stay on a regular schedule.
- Build in time for relaxation and needed rest.
- Exercise daily.
- Watch your diet. Excess fat, sugar, and caffeine can make depression worse.
- Spend time with encouraging friends. Being with loved ones makes the day brighter.
- Volunteer to help someone less fortunate.
- Count your blessings. Think about the true meaning of the Season.

We can overcome the "simple blues" and be better people and a blessing to others as we do. Be a blessing and be blessed!

There are no limits to caring ®

December 21

The earth, O LORD, is full of your steadfast love; teach me your
statutes

(Psalm 119:64, ESV)

Wrapping Paper

After coming home from a long day at work, a father was angered to see that his young daughter had used all of the family's roll of expensive wrapping paper. He worked very hard just to keep food on the table and now would have to find a way to get more wrapping paper.

On Christmas Eve, he noticed the box under the tree…empty. This angered him even more. Christmas morning, the excited little girl ran up to her father with the box and said, "This is for you, Daddy!"

He opened the box but found nothing inside. He said, "All it is is an empty box!" Looking up at him, with tears in her eyes she said, "It's not empty. I blew kisses in it until it was all full."

Are we missing the precious moments with others because we only see or think inside the box? Look for the deeper meaning of life and relationships this holiday season.

There are no limits to caring ®

December 22

Let your light shine before others, that they may see your good deeds and glorify your Father in heaven (Matthew 5:16, NIV).

Jacob

Unexpectedly, 8-year-old Jacob Creel died right before Christmas. His parents were shocked and grieved. They couldn't believe that their only child had died. Now it was Christmas, and suddenly, his mother realized that Jacob would not be opening the gifts that were already under the tree. What now?

You see, Jacob was full of the spirit of giving. His mother said she recently fussed at him for returning home without his shirt. He explained he'd given it to a friend because he wanted one just like it.

Knowing Jacob as they did, his parents said, "Jacob would want his gifts to go to children in need."

Some of his gifts have since gone to a little boy and girl whose father is awaiting a new heart. Now, this family has a small piece of Jacob's heart.

Jacob found a way to continue to bless others. You too can find a way!

There are no limits to caring ®

December 23

*But the angel said to them, "Do not be afraid. I bring you good
news that will cause great joy for all the people*
(Luke 2:10, NIV).

Joy

Jane appeared older than her thirty-five years. Her eyes were dull,
shoulders slumped, and spirits low. She had witnessed the
disappearance of her dreams, the death of her husband, the
desertion of her friends, and the collapse of her health. As she
paused to listen to a church choir sing, "*Joy to the World*," she
remarked, "Joy is a luxury I can't afford."

Does the Christmas message have anything to say to the Janes of
our world? Is there really joy for all people? What can we say to
those around us who are suffering?

Maybe we should speak with actions more than words. And then,
we can all find joy. We, who have been blessed, must be a blessing
to others.

Join us at Volunteers of America this Christmas, by sharing acts of
joy. Call us and see how you, your business, school, church, or
civic group can help.

There are no limits to caring ®

370

December 24

For to us a child is born, to us a son is given, and the government will be on his shoulders. And he will be called Wonderful Counselor, Mighty God, Everlasting Father, Prince of Peace (Isaiah 9:6, NIV).

The Christmas Truce

It was Christmas Eve, 1941, and England and Germany were in the midst of World War I. Around midnight, on Christmas Eve, the fighting stopped.

Early Christmas morning, German soldiers came out of their trenches and approached the Allied soldiers, calling "Merry Christmas." The Allied soldiers were uncertain, thinking it was a trick. But they soon left their trenches and shook hands with the German soldiers.

Troops decorated their trenches for Christmas, and the two sides began singing Christmas carols. The German and English soldiers exchanged small gifts. For the moment, there was no war.

The truce lasted through Christmas night, and in some areas, it continued until New Year's Day.

Christmas time inspires us all to think of others, to speak kind words, to laugh more, and to give more. We forget our differences and come together to celebrate this special day. Why? Because we remember a small child born in Bethlehem, who came to bring each of us peace.

There are no limits to caring ®

December 25

For unto you is born this day in the city of David a Savior, who is
Christ the Lord (Luke 2:11, ESV).

Merry Christmas

Great speeches live on. Roosevelt said, "The only thing we have to fear is fear itself!" Kennedy challenged us: "Ask not what your country can do for you, ask what *you* can do for your country!" Or Reagan, "Tear down this wall!" Those speeches will live on. But the greatest speech was given over 2000 years ago, in a small, secluded town called Bethlehem, *"For unto you is born this day in the city of David, a Savior, who is Christ the Lord."*

The subject of that speech is the reason for this season. That subject was love and peace. Today, we celebrate the love and peace that Jesus brought into the world.

Jesus came to take away fear, to teach us to give, and to tear down walls that divide us. Joy to the world, the Lord has come.

We at VOA wish you a Merry Christmas and hope that you and your family will have the joy of Christmas—the joy that comes from giving out of gratitude.

There are no limits to caring ®

December 26

... God loves people who love to give (2 Corinthians 9:7, CEV).

Christmas Gifts

Well, did you get what you wanted for Christmas? A better question: Did you GIVE what you wanted to give this year? Did you run out of cash, or time, or gift ideas before Christmas?

Here are some gift ideas that do not require cash. And, they would be welcome at any time of the year.

- Tell someone, "I love you."
- Give a word of encouragement.
- Forgive someone who has wronged you.
- Apologize to someone you have wronged.
- Show kindness to a co-worker.
- Spend time with your family. They need it.

Well, you get it. Those kinds of gifts can actually be the most meaningful of all. Those gifts change lives. They are needed and welcomed by everyone, at any time of the year. Be a blessing to others!

There are no limits to caring ®

December 27

*Anxiety in a man's heart weighs him down, but a good word
makes him glad* (Proverbs 12:25, ESV).

Hot Down Here

A man left the icy streets of Chicago for a vacation in Florida. His wife was on a business trip and was planning to meet him in Florida the next day.

When he reached his hotel, he decided to send his wife a quick email. Unable to find her email address, he did his best to type it in from memory. Unfortunately, he missed one letter and his note was directed instead to an elderly preacher's wife whose husband had just passed away only the day before.

When the grieving preacher's widow checked her email, she saw the monitor, let out a scream, and fainted. Her family rushed into the room and saw this note on the screen: "Dearest wife, just got checked in. Everything ready for your arrival tomorrow. P.S. Sure is hot down here!"

Even with modern gadgets, communication is a challenge. But good communication is so important with our spouses, our children, it's worth the effort.

There are no limits to caring ®

December 28

Let the wise hear and increase in learning, and the one who understands obtain guidance (Proverbs 1:5, ESV).

Snow Today

One winter morning, Joe and his wife heard the radio announcer say, "We are going to have 8 inches of snow today. Please park your car on the even-numbered side of the street, so the snowplow can get through." So, Joe went out and moved his car.

A week later, they heard a similar announcement, asking residents to please park their cars on the odd-numbered side of the street. So, Joe went out and moved his car.

The next week, the same kind of announcement came on the radio. But before they could hear which side of the street to park on, the power went out. Joe said, "Well, I don't know which side of the street to park on."

His wife gently suggested, "Honey, why don't you just leave the car in the garage this time."

Sometimes, we just don't get it. And sometimes, we need help to see it. And sometimes, we need to offer help—gently.

There are no limits to caring ®

December 29

Not getting what you want can break your heart, but a wish that comes true is a life-giving tree (Proverbs 13:2, CEV).

Expectations

Anna Grace is a normal 4-year-old girl, who likes to play and who loves her family. She is very active, full of energy, and enjoys going to school.

Knowing that Anna Grace loves fried chicken, I picked some up and brought it to her at our house, where she was playing. After she realized what I had brought her, she said, "Papa, I won't get mad, but did you bring me 4 pieces of chicken or 6 pieces of chicken?" She had expectations for 6 pieces of chicken, but she was ok if her expectations were not met.

What happens when you don't get what you want? Get mad? Get even? What we do when we don't get what we want is always our choice.

How we respond to unmet expectations makes all the difference. Perhaps we could follow the example of Anna Grace... "I won't get mad if I don't get what I want!" I like Anna Grace's choice ...Choose a positive alternative to anger.

Anna Grace, have some fried chicken today!

December 30

*The end of a matter is better than its beginning, and patience is
better than pride* (Ecclesiastes 7:8, NIV).

Ending

How we finish may be remembered more than anything else in our lives. During his second presidential campaign, Abraham Lincoln responded to Grace Bedell, an 11-year-old girl who had written to the President saying that she would try to persuade her four brothers to vote for him, if he grew a beard.

Lincoln wrote back, "My dear little Miss...As to the whiskers, having never worn any, do you not think people would call it a piece of silly affection if I were to begin now?"

Lincoln began his beard just a few years before his death. We rarely see a picture of him without a beard. We remember him the way he finished.

How do you want to be remembered? As a caring person? Since we never know when we will finish our course, we need to be the way we want to be remembered at all times. Just think. The impression you make today could last forever.

December 31

Oh sing to the LORD a new song, for he has done marvelous things!
(Psalm 98:1, ESV).

Starting Over

Yogi Berra said, "If I had to do it all over again, I'd do it all over again." Well, we think we know what he meant to say. But would we want to do it all over again the same way, or would we want to make some changes? There are probably some things we would not want to repeat. While we cannot repeat the past, we can do something about the future.

Today can be a day of starting over. A day to do better at a job, or a relationship. A day to move from self-interest to interest in others. A day in which you can reach out and make a positive difference in the life of another person.

We cannot go back, but we can move forward. We can't change the past, but we can make some changes in today! After all, tomorrow is not only a new day, but a New Year!

There are no limits to caring ®

378

There are no limits to caring ®

About the Author

Wallace T. Davis is a graduate of Samford University and New Orleans Baptist Theological Seminary with a Bachelor of Science in Education, a Master of Theology, and a Doctor of Philosophy in Psychology and Counseling.

Wallace served as pastor, teacher, counselor, keynote speaker, and Chief Executive Officer, spanning over 50 years. For 42 years, he has been with Volunteers of America. In 1980, with the founding of Volunteers of America in Mobile, he became the first Community Board President and, shortly afterwards, the first Executive Director. As President and Chief Executive Officer, he led the organization to expand and serve Alabama, Georgia, and Mississippi addressing some of the most challenging spiritual, social, and economic issues of our time.

Wallace and his wife Barbara have four adult children and nine grandchildren.

There are no limits to caring ®

Permissions for Bible Translations Used

There are no limits to caring ®

There are no limits to caring ®